THE
Pearlmaker

THE

Pearlmaker

Jim AND Judson Cornwall

WORD PUBLISHING

Word (UK) Ltd
Milton Keynes, England

WORD AUSTRALIA
Kilsyth, Victoria, Australia

STRUIK CHRISTIAN BOOKS (PTY) LTD
Maitland, South Africa

JOINT DISTRIBUTORS SINGAPORE –
ALBY COMMERCIAL ENTERPRISES PTE LTD
and
CAMPUS CRUSADE

CHRISTIAN MARKETING NEW ZEALAND LTD
Havelock North, New Zealand

JENSCO LTD
Hong Kong

SALVATION BOOK CENTRE
Malaysia

THE PEARLMAKER

Copyright © 1992 by Jim and Judson Cornwall.

First published in the USA by Creation House, a division of Strang Communications Company, Lake Mary, Florida.

First UK edition, Nelson Word Ltd., Milton Keynes, 1993.

ISBN 0-85009-592-1   (Australia ISBN 1-86258-274-2)

Unless otherwise indicated, Scripture quotations are from the King James Version of the Bible.

Scripture quotations marked AMP are from the Amplified Bible. Old Testament copyright © 1965,1987 by the Zondervan Corporation. The Amplified New Testament copyright © 1954, 1958, 1987 by the Lockman Foundation. Used by permission.

Scripture quotations marked NKJV are from the New King James Version of the Bible. Copyright © 1979, 1980, 1982 by Thomas Nelson Inc., publishers. Used by permission.

Scripture quotations marked TCNT are from the Twentieth Century New Testament. Copyright © 1900, 1901, 1902, 1903, 1904 by Fleming H. Revell, London and Edinburgh.

Scripture quotations marked Weymouth are from the New Testament in Modern Speech paraphrased by Richard Francis Weymouth. Copyright © 1929, 1932, 1936, 1937, 1939, 1940, 1941 by the Pilgrim Press, Cleveland, Ohio. Used by permission.

Reproduced, printed and bound in Great Britain for Nelson Word Ltd. by Cox and Wyman Ltd., Reading.

93 94 95 96 / 10 9 8 7 6 5 4 3 2 1

*To my loving wife, Suzy, who is my best friend,
my faithful companion and my partner in ministry.
She has lived out the experiences with me
that are shared in this book, and through them
we have learned together the principles of God.*

CONTENTS

PREFACE

AS A FORMER businessman, I am accustomed to conducting business over lunch meetings. But when my oldest brother, Judson, and I have lunch together, it is strictly for fellowship. He is my spiritual mentor, and I treat our lunches like a class in Bible school. One day when we were having lunch I raised a question about the gates of pearl in the walls of the New Jerusalem. Little did I realize that our discussion would develop into a book.

A few months later Judson told me that what we had discussed was enlarging in his mind and that he thought there was a book there someplace. I told him to "go for it," and, knowing how quickly he sketches out a book, I thought he would start working on it immediately. He didn't. Instead, when we would get together, he would continue to discuss the idea with me further. I repeatedly told him to write a book on it. Instead of doing so, he wrote five other books while we were talking about these gates of pearl.

I was surprised, almost to the point of shock, when he said that he felt the book was actually mine and that I should write it. I was far too busy pastoring to write. This didn't discourage him. He simply said that he would help me.

Now, months later, I am thrilled to see my concepts in writing, and I look forward to seeing them shared with the body of Christ that reaches far beyond my local church. We have all experienced life's painful irritants and the suffering they bring. But we seldom realize what the life of Christ within us can do with those painful irritants. The world says, "When stuck with lemons, make lemonade!" Jesus offers something far greater. When pierced with irritants, He becomes a pearlmaker. So can we.

It is my prayer that more and more Christians will make pearls to present to the Master.

Jim Cornwall
Phoenix, Arizona
1992

CHAPTER ONE

POSITIVE RESULTS FROM LIFE'S IRRITATIONS

IT MUST HAVE BEEN Monday because nothing was going right. Secure in the sandy sediment where the river met the ocean, Marvin the mollusk gently opened his shell to suck in sea water, just as he had done all his life. Yet this time the water running though his filter system left a sharp grain of sand in his body that he could not dislodge. Nothing that had ever worked before would cause this particle of silica to leave. While the sand wasn't life-threatening, it was very irritating. His day was absolutely ruined.

After a couple of days it became obvious that this grain of sand was there for the long haul. It was wedged between the soft flesh of the oyster and its outer shell. Marvin's every movement accentuated this irritation, similar to the way a pebble in a shoe creates increasing pain the farther one walks.

Obviously, however, oysters and humans handle irritations quite differently. We can remove our shoe and extract the pebble, but the oyster cannot unclothe itself to get to the grain of sand. Therefore God has provided the oyster with a special secretion called *nacre* (nay-kur). Much as a spider expels material to spin into a web, the oyster can secrete nacre around the irritant to make it less bothersome.

With inherent, God-given instinct, Marvin formed a protective sac around the foreign substance and then systematically covered the sand with this secretion. This dulled the sharp edges, but the sand still put pressure against his flesh. So he released more secretion and gave the sand a second coating. This was followed by layer after layer of nacre. Months turned into years, but the irritation would not go away. Although it was now smooth and round and did not cut anymore, it was growing in size until the mollusk felt as if someone were pressing a finger in his side.

Marvin felt defeated. In spite of all his hard work, the irritant had only become larger. He was certain this immense growth made him an abnormality. "No one will ever want me," he moaned. When the oyster harvester's rake pulled Marvin from his home in the sediment, there was no resistance. Depression had replaced the delight of life. What can happen that is any worse than these past seven years of suffering have been? he thought.

The next morning the oyster shucker cut the muscle that held the two halves of the shell together and slid the oyster into a bowl. The room exploded with an excited scream: "Look what I found! It's the largest pearl I've ever seen. It's worth a fortune!" The way that oyster handled its pain became the source of another's pleasure.

The pearl is the only gem that is formed by a living organism, and it is, therefore, the most fragile of them all. Pearls scratch easily and will begin to dissolve when they come in contact with acid. Other gems are the result of sediment or carbon that has undergone extreme heat and pressure in the bowels of the earth. While all gems have commercial value, a large, perfect pearl that developed in an oyster without human manipulation can command a greater price than a well-cut diamond.

When speaking to merchants, Jesus told of one:

> Who, when he had found one pearl of great price, went and sold all that he had, and bought it (Matthew 13:46).

Whether we see this merchant as ourselves discovering salvation or Christ redeeming His church, this parable demonstrates the value pearls have had since antiquity.

When we come to the end of the Bible, John, the revelator, paints us a descriptive picture of the New Jerusalem. He describes the foundation as twelve massive gemstones in which are carved the names of the twelve apostles (see Revelation 21:14,19). He further says that the walls of the city are pure jasper and the city itself is pure gold as transparent as glass (see Revelation 21:18). By these descriptions we know that the walls and city of the New Jerusalem are mineral by nature. Then, rather peculiarly, John says:

> And the twelve gates were twelve pearls: every several gate was of one pearl (Revelation 21:21).

Two years ago while Judson and I were having lunch together, I asked him, "Why would God use fragile pearls as the gates to a city made of solid gemstones?" Several rather obvious answers came out of that conversation:

1. Their iridescent beauty. Ancient gates were often very ornamental.

2. Their high value. Gates were highly treasured as the security of the city.

3. Their fragile nature. These gates are never closed so their strength is not an issue.

4. Their unique origins. Pearls are formed by living organisms in response to irritants.

This fourth point caught our attention. We also knew by what John wrote in Revelation 21 that the gates were the only entrance to the New Jerusalem. Could it be that these gates are symbolic of Jesus?

Consider what Jesus says in the book of John:

> I am the way, the truth, and the life: no man cometh unto the Father, but by me...Verily, verily, I say unto you, I am the door of the sheep...He that entereth not by the door into the sheepfold, but climbeth up some other way, the same is a thief and a robber (John 14:6; 10:7; 10:1).

The author of the book of Hebrews further assures us there is but one entrance to heaven, that being Jesus:

> Having therefore, brethren, boldness to enter into the holiest by the blood of Jesus, by a new and living way, which he hath conse-crated for us, through the veil, that is to say, his flesh...Let us draw near with a true heart (Hebrews 10:19-20,22).

In the same way that Christ ushers us into the pres-ence of God, Christ has become the gates of the New Jerusalem, the only means of entrance into the city. He is available as three entrances on each of the four sides of the city, so the trinity of the Godhead is evident to all who enter therein.

Look at the word *consecrated* in the verses I quoted earlier from Hebrews 10. The original Greek for that word is *egkainizo*, which means "to renew" or "to inaugurate." The oyster does this with a grain of sand. It renews or "makes new" the sand. The oyster uses the sand to inaugurate the production of a pearl. Christ has consecrated (or set aside) a living way into God's presence. All access to the Father is through the Son, Jesus Christ. Jesus told Nathanael:

> Verily, verily, I say unto you, Hereafter ye shall see heaven open, and the angels of God ascending and descending upon the Son of man (John 1:51).

Jesus is the route of access from earth to heaven as well as from heaven to earth. Angels and men traverse this route. Jesus declared:

> I am the door: by me if any man enter in, he shall be saved, and shall go in and out, and find pasture (John 10:9).

John the apostle saw and entered that doorway to heaven, for he wrote:

> After this I looked, and, behold, a door was opened in heaven: and the first voice which I heard was as it were of a trumpet talking with me; which said, Come up hither, and I will shew thee things which must be hereafter (Revelation 4:1).

11

As Judson and I further discussed the pearly doorways into heaven, an obvious question came to mind: Where would pearls that *big* come from? After all, the city walls were twelve thousand furlongs — fifteen hundred miles — tall! We concluded that in a symbolic sense Jesus may well have produced these giant pearls the same way an oyster would — by His response to irritation in His life. Jesus covered the nuisances in His life with God's grace until they figuratively became pearls large enough for the walls of the New Jerusalem. Those would be some pearls! But then, He is some Christ!

The apostle John made the amazing observation, "As he is, so are we in this world" (1 John 4:17). This does not, of course, make gods of any of us. It merely affirms that what happened to Jesus will happen to us. Jesus told His disciples:

> Remember the word that I said unto you, The servant is not greater than his lord. If they have persecuted me, they will also persecute you; if they have kept my saying, they will keep yours also (John 15:20).

Jesus came not only as our redeemer but also as our pattern. Christ never intended His death at Calvary to exempt us from tests, trials and temptations. He died to enable us to endure them while victoriously producing priceless pearls to lay at His feet when we enter heaven's gates.

Our soft generation has gladly embraced a theology of escapism. We love to hear preachers tell us that Jesus doesn't want us to have grains of sand in our lives. Somehow these proclaimers have ignored Paul's admonition:

Be not thou therefore ashamed of the testimony of our Lord, nor of me his prisoner: but be thou partaker of the afflictions of the gospel according to the power of God (2 Timothy 1:8).

Some preachers deliberately ignore Peter's urging:

Beloved, think it not strange concerning the fiery trial which is to try you, as though some strange thing happened unto you: But rejoice, inasmuch as ye are partakers of Christ's sufferings; that, when his glory shall be revealed, ye may be glad also with exceeding joy (1 Peter 4:12-13).

Peter seemed convinced that "all that will live godly in Christ Jesus shall suffer persecution" (2 Timothy 3:12). He had observed this in Jesus and had experienced it in his own life. Friends of his had been killed for their testimony, and later he too would suffer martyrdom. Peter did not present suffering as something to which we aspire. He merely stated it as a matter of fact: suffering will be part of our lives if we are truly disciples of Christ.

Perhaps as an overreaction to the teaching of escapism, other preachers are proclaiming holiness through suffering. This teaching has reintroduced the doctrine of asceticism which views the body as unholy, the mind as impure and the senses as evil. Asceticism teaches that having nothing is pure; suffering is holy; and weeping, remorse and expressed sorrow are righteous. It seems to have replaced the joy of the Lord with sorrow of soul. It substitutes misery for pleasure and spiritual insecurity for our glorious hope.

Both escapism and asceticism are dangerous extremes, and one does not balance out the other. The New Testament teaches us that Christ came that we might have life, peace, hope and joy. The heart of the gospel is well-being and right relationships both with God and with people. But this does not exempt us from the harsh realities of life on earth. Jesus told His disciples:

> These things I have spoken unto you, that in me ye might have peace. In the world ye shall have tribulation: but be of good cheer; I have overcome the world (John 16:33).

This is not speaking of escaping *from* trouble but escaping *in the midst of* trouble through faith in Jesus Christ.

Rather than exempt us from the irritants of life, Jesus has shown us how to overcome them completely. In comparing Christians to soldiers, Paul tells us:

> Thou therefore endure hardness, as a good soldier of Jesus Christ (2 Timothy 2:3).

A soldier's training involves boot camp, forced marches and long hours. A time of glory may come in a soldier's future, but many hours of tedium, tension and training will come before it. Should we Christians expect to be victorious soldiers without similar training? The privation, pain and penalties that are experienced following enlistment are not the goals of any soldier. They are merely the means to an end. They are the grains of sand that cause the oysters to produce pearls.

Similarly, it should not come as a surprise when fiery trials ravage our lives. Soldiers are not needed if there is no enemy. Our Christian lives will be challenged —

some more vigorously than others, but not all of these tests and trials come from the devil. Tests and temptations come from at least five major sources:

1. God Himself tests His saints to reveal the great strength He has instilled within them.

2. Christian brothers and sisters can be the cause of frustration in our lives.

3. Our worldly associates, who do not understand our relationship with Jesus, will try our faith and consecration daily.

4. We often produce our own worst temptations. James 1:14 tells us: "But every man is tempted, when he is drawn away of his own lust, and enticed."

5. The pain of daily living often results in severe trial.

Some of the most vigorous irritations that enter our lives have no spiritual foundation at all. They come as the natural outgrowth of living. Sickness, financial reverses, war, natural disasters, fire and so forth afflict the saint as well as the sinner. As Solomon observed:

> All things come alike to all: there is one
> event to the righteous, and to the wicked; to
> the good and to the clean, and to the unclean;
> to him that sacrificeth, and to him that sacri-
> ficeth not: as is the good, so is the sinner; and
> he that sweareth, as he that feareth an oath
> (Ecclesiastes 9:2).

Solomon believed that righteousness was not automatic exemption from the negative forces in life. Does this nullify the virtue of living a righteous life of faith? Of course not! Righteousness and holy living have rewards for the present built into them, and they also carry with them glorious compensation for the future. But righteousness does not immunize us against the harsh realities of living on this planet. Ask the Hebrew children as they tumbled into the fiery furnace. God could have prevented them from being thrown into the furnace for refusing to worship the golden image Nebuchadnezzar had built, but He didn't. He chose to give these men an opportunity to produce pearls. Since then millions of believers have been encouraged and challenged to renewed faith as they read of the absolute resolve of these three men to serve Jehovah — whatever the cost — and of the "fourth man in the fire."

In the New Testament, we can check with the apostle Paul about immunity to suffering as he spent long, lonely hours chained in crude prison cells. God could have halted the nearly ceaseless persecution this apostle suffered, but He didn't. Instead He enabled him to go through the suffering and produce priceless gems for the rest of us to admire. Our New Testament would be about half its size if Paul hadn't become a pearlmaker by using his prison time to write his epistles. This served to ease the pain of his temporal suffering, and once written the epistles became timeless pearls that have adorned the lives of countless Christians.

Perhaps modern Christians should not lose faith so quickly when apparent reversals come. More important than positions, possessions and power in this life is the production of something that we can present to Jesus when we meet Him in the air. Furthermore, as Solomon wisely observed:

> As he came forth of his mother's womb, naked shall he return to go as he came, and shall take nothing of his labour, which he may carry away in his hand (Ecclesiastes 5:15).

Not all oysters produce pearls; less than ten percent of them do. Usually they are successful in flushing the sand from their systems. When they cannot get rid of the irritant, some adjust to the pain while others make a pearl of it. Similarly, not all Christians endure affliction and trials, but those who do undergo the severity of testing have a glorious opportunity to make a pearl out of it.

We have deliberately chosen twelve incidents from the Gospels that seemed to have been major irritants in the life of Jesus, and these will form the backbone of this book. Christ handled each irritation in such a way that could have produced the magnificent pearl gates of the New Jerusalem. Our approach will not be strictly historical because Jesus still lives His life within us. Instead we will compare His irritations to irritants in our own lives. If we allow the life of Christ within us to cover these foreign invasions, we can be certain that His life will form a pearl of beauty within us.

Suffering can either produce resentment and bitterness or pearls of great beauty. A Christlike response to suffering won't necessarily bring an end to it, but the Savior's indwelling life can turn distressing circumstances into gem-making opportunities. O

CHAPTER TWO

THE IRRITATION OF THE HUMAN BODY

CHRISTMAS WAS ALWAYS the highlight of the year when I was growing up. Although my father was a pastor who survived the depression and continued to live on a very low budget, my parents always made Christmas a festive season. I look back now on my childhood Christmases with two regrets: First, I was not mature enough to value some of the gifts. I never prized clothing as a present. I wanted playthings, but long after the toy was broken or set aside, I wore the clothes. Second, I lament that I did not appreciate how much it cost my parents to provide the Christmas celebration for the family. It was not simply a December expense to them. They had saved all year long for this time of gift giving.

Now as I prepare to lead my congregation into the Christmas season, I fear that, like myself as a boy, these people neither fully esteem the value of God's gift nor appreciate the costly nature of God's Christmas present. Some people approach Jesus as a sort of spiritual toy, but Jesus did not come to accommodate our pleasure. He is the difference between life and death for us. He Himself declared:

> I am come that they might have life, and that they might have it more abundantly (John 10:10).

God's gift at Bethlehem was the gift of life. Much as parents give life to their children, so God has given us life in His Son. All other gifts become useful because of this life.

This gift of God is freely received, but it is not free. Jesus paid a tremendous price to become our Christmas gift. Not being God, we cannot fully appreciate what it meant to set divinity aside to take on humanity, but that is what happened at the birth of Jesus. He who had always existed submitted willingly to a beginning through gestation in Mary's womb. Christ, who had always been Spirit, now was entombed in human flesh. The unlimitedness of the Godhead was exchanged for the extreme limitations of a human being.

We can never measure the depth of love that caused Christ to agree to become a man. Even our most learned theologians are unable to explain such divine love satisfactorily, but the humblest child can experience it. Only divine wisdom could have conceived a redemptive plan that begins with the incarnation. The coming of Jesus was designed before the foundations of the world were laid. Every aspect of the incarnation was carefully planned. As the writer of the epistle to the Hebrews said:

> Wherefore when he cometh into the world, he saith, Sacrifice and offering thou wouldest

not, but a body hast thou prepared me...Then said he, Lo, I come to do thy will, O God. He taketh away the first, that he may establish the second (Hebrews 10:5,9).

God provided His Son a body that would die because He was to become the eternal sacrifice for the sins of mankind, and "the wages of sin is death" (Romans 6:23). Angels cannot die, so Jesus could not successfully take on the form of an angel. Only mortals die, so Jesus took on mortality. He became what we are in order to enable us to become what He is. It was a costly trade-off for Him but a crowning trade-up for us.

The Scriptures teach incontrovertibly that Jesus was the Son of God, and as such He was and is a part of the Godhead — Father, Son, Holy Spirit. When theologians seek to define God's nature, they generally speak of His omniscience (all knowing), omnipresence (present everywhere), omnipotence (all powerful), and eternity (He always was, now is and shall ever be). All of this had to be voluntarily laid aside when the Christ of God became Jesus, the man.

The theologians call this the *kenosis* — a Greek word meaning self-emptying. In his letter to the church at Philippi, Paul describes this release of the divine in order to become human. The Amplified New Testament puts it this way:

Who, [Jesus] although being essentially one with God and in the form of God [possessing the fullness of the attributes which make God God], did not think this equality with God was a thing to be eagerly grasped or retained; But stripped Himself [of all privileges and rightful dignity] so as to assume the guise of

> a servant (slave), in that He became like men
> and was born a human being (Philippians
> 2:6-7).

The angels shouted, the shepherds wondered and the wise men worshipped at the birth of Jesus; but the babe lying in the manger must have been bewildered. He knew nothing of His past, had no idea of His future and could relate to His present in only the most immature fashion. God was now a baby.

Jesus never ceased to be God. He merely "stripped Himself [of all privileges and rightful dignity] so as to assume the guise of a servant." It may have been somewhat like losing access to a program on the computer. You know it is on the disk, but you cannot call it up. Isn't it likely that somewhere in the depth of Jesus' nature there was an inner awareness of something greater than His boyhood? It was this "something" that responded so enthusiastically to the teaching in the synagogue that He lost track of time for three days and failed to go home with His parents (see Luke 2:49).

Not until His baptism in water did Jesus have any outside confirmation of what He had come to believe in His spirit. John the Baptist publicly announced Him as the "Lamb of God, which taketh away the sin of the world" (John 1:29), and the voice of the Father spoke from heaven proclaiming Jesus to be "my beloved Son" (see Mark 1:11). Nothing Satan could do to Him in the wilderness temptation could shake His conviction that He was the God-man sent to be the Savior of the world.

The thirty-three years that Jesus lived on earth as a man were filled with irritations, but none could have been more flagrant than being incarcerated in a human body. He who had been omniscient, possessing all knowledge about all things, had to learn to walk, talk, feed himself and read and write. He had to learn and grow in knowledge like the rest of us. Dr. Luke tells us:

> And the child grew, and waxed strong in spirit, filled with wisdom: and the grace of God was upon him...And Jesus increased in wisdom and stature, and in favour with God and man (Luke 2:40,52).

Jesus actually had to discover things that He had originally created. He was dependent upon the inspiration of the Holy Spirit to know information that He had inherently known before the incarnation. This must have been as irritating to Him as the loss of memory is to aging persons. They have an awareness that they should know certain information, but they cannot pull it back to the conscious mind.

Jesus had to function within the limitations forced upon Him by this loss of omniscience. He who had always known all things through eternity now found His knowledge limited to what had been put into His mind —much as a computer cannot give out what has not been programmed in. On repeated occasions, we see Jesus asking questions of His disciples concerning natural things. He, the Teacher, was asking information from the students. He also spent long nights communicating with the Father in prayer, and that enabled Him to understand all He needed to know in order to have a fruitful ministry. He testified:

> I can of mine own self do nothing: as I hear, I judge: and my judgment is just; because I seek not mine own will, but the will of the Father which hath sent me (John 5:30).

Jesus had to depend upon the Father's knowledge and wisdom while He was entombed in human flesh. Much as the oyster secretes nacre around the irritating sand, Jesus surrounded the irritation of His limited knowledge with much communion with the unlimited Father. What He lacked, the Father possessed and shared with the Son.

While entombed in a human body, Jesus was equally separated from His essential nature of omnipresence. As God He had been present everywhere, but while He lived on earth He was confined to one geographic location at a time.

For us mobile Americans, it is difficult to realize just how restricted Jesus actually was. He was born in an obscure country occupied by the Roman army, and during the time of His ministry He never traveled as far as some people travel today just to go to work. He had to walk wherever He went. He didn't even have access to a horse or a donkey except for the brief ride into Jerusalem on Palm Sunday. This had to be an aggravation to Him.

Judson tells me that one of the aggravations of his traveling ministry is being confined to a motel. He surrenders the freedom of his own car by flying to a city, and from that point on, he goes whenever and wherever the pastor chooses to take him. How much greater was the loss of freedom for Jesus. In one divine action, He both lost the unlimited access to everywhere that He had always known and gained such access as walking could provide for Him. That had to be irritating to Jesus.

Christ's omnipotence was also laid aside when He left heaven. He who had always been able to do anything and everything was now limited to the technology and intelligence of His generation.

If jet transportation had been available to Him, He

could have ministered in many countries of the world. If television had been invented, He could have preached to the people of the world from Nazareth. He didn't even have a public address system to help Him speak to the vast crowds that followed Him.

As the man Jesus, He could not function as the Creator. He was absolutely dependent upon the Father's power for everything He did. By taking on the form of a man, He laid aside His omnipotence. He told the Jewish religious leaders:

> The Son can do nothing of himself, but what he seeth the Father do: for what things soever he doeth, these also doeth the Son likewise (John 5:19).

By accepting the limitations of the human body He was setting an example for us. He told His disciples:

> Verily, verily, I say unto you, He that believeth on me, the works that I do shall he do also; and greater works than these shall he do; because I go unto my Father (John 14:12).

He ministered here on earth without possessing omnipotence or omniscience, and so can we. The success of His ministry was directly linked to His belief in God's unlimitedness, and He gave us that same access to God through prayer and the indwelling Holy Spirit.

The four Gospels show us that Jesus obviously did more miracles than anyone before Him had done, and He performed at least one miracle that no one else had ever done — opening blind eyes. Yet none of these miracles was wrought by inherent power. He derived all of

His power and authority from God the Father.

Just as surely as Jesus laid aside His divine attributes of omniscience, omnipresence and omnipotence, He also stepped from eternity into time when He was born in Bethlehem of Judea. He who had been without beginning or end was now to experience both of them. He could not have helped being irritated at time limitations. He had but three and a half years to fulfill His ministry. He lived with a constant awareness that His death was imminent. When time is short, everything seems to take longer than necessary, and that is irritating.

Jesus came on a short mission, but He was stripped of His divine tools of unlimited knowledge, power, proximity and timelessness. It had to be a pressing irritant to Him.

This human body not only greatly limited Him, but it made demands upon Him that were new to Him. He felt hunger — something totally unknown in heaven. He also experienced exhaustion. At one time He grew so weary that He sat outside a city at the public well waiting for His disciples to go into the town to buy food for Him to eat. He always yearned to introduce the Father to the people, but He had physical limitations just as we do.

Physical exhaustion must have been a continual irritant to Jesus, for there seemed to be no end to the needs of the people who came to Him, yet His body demanded rest. Similarly, the hunger pangs interrupted His thought patterns when He was teaching. Surely when the multitude was faint for lack of food, Jesus must have been experiencing something comparable in His own body. Dare we think that His body didn't complain when He knelt in prayer out in the countryside? Have any of us gone to prayer without having to fight our physical being?

Undoubtedly Jesus shivered in the cold of the night and suffered in the heat of the day. He never discredited His body. He took proper care of it. He probably joined David in saying:

> For You formed my inward parts; You cov-
> ered me in my mother's womb. I will praise
> You, for I am fearfully and wonderfully
> made; marvelous are Your works, and that
> my soul knows very well (Psalm 139:13-14,
> NKJV).

Still, for all the wonder of the human body, we have been made "a little lower than the angels" (Psalm 8:5), and the writer to the Hebrews doubly emphasizes this in saying:

> But we see Jesus, who was made a little
> lower than the angels for the suffering of
> death, crowned with glory and honor; that he
> by the grace of God should taste death for
> every man (Hebrews 2:9).

It had to be irritating for the Creator to be limited to a body lower than the lowest angel in heaven. But Jesus did not fight it, complain about it or withdraw from ministering because of it. Like the oyster, He encompassed the irritation in a sac and poured the nacre of dependence upon God around it.

Regardless of how long we may have been Christians, and irrespective of the spiritual maturity we may have achieved, all of us are irritated by our human bodies. Not only do we experience fatigue, hunger, sleeplessness, cold and heat; we suffer pain, sickness and disease.

While we have never known omniscience, we live with a limitation of knowledge. Fortunately one of the gifts of the Holy Spirit is a "word of knowledge through the same Spirit" (1 Corinthians 12:8). Like Jesus, we can cover the irritation of our inherent ignorance through natural learning and through receiving special words of knowledge from God.

Even though we are limited to being in only one place at a time, we can be in the divine omnipresence through fellowship with God in prayer, for His promise is:

> My presence shall go with thee, and I will give thee rest (Exodus 33:14).

If the Bible has one consistent theme, it is the availability of the presence of God for the believer who desires it. It will form a powerful layer of spiritual nacre around the irritant of the human body's limitations. When we become irritated with our personal inabilities, we can find a covering protection in the repeated promises of Jesus that He will share His power with us. He said:

> Behold, I give unto you power to tread on serpents and scorpions, and over all the power of the enemy: and nothing shall by any means hurt you (Luke 10:19).

The Christian's power over the enemy is always conferred power (given by God), which means it is always more than sufficient. The gospel is a powerful gospel, and God's children have access to a powerful God. The more we remain in His presence, the more consistently His power covers the irritant of our inherent impotence.

Whether consciously or subconsciously, the major irritant of living in a human body is our lack of eternity. We know that we are appointed to death from the moment of our birth. We are surrounded by dying people, and it brings us face to face with our mortality. Some people live in such fear of death that they die a hundred deaths a day. As Solomon wisely declared:

> He has put eternity in their hearts, except that no one can find out the work that God does from beginning to end (Ecclesiastes 3:11, NKJV).

All of our hearts hold a touch of eternity. Even the self-proclaimed atheist has an inner awareness that life does not cease when the body dies. This awareness of the eternity of the soul is a serious irritation to many people. When we reach out to touch eternity through worshipping God, we can cover the irritation with the reality of the hope God has laid up for us in His eternity. Jesus promised His disciples and us:

> And if I go and prepare a place for you, I will come again, and receive you unto myself; that where I am, there ye may be also (John 14:3).

He further told the Father in His high-priestly prayer:

> Father, I will that they also, whom thou hast given me, be with me where I am; that they may behold my glory, which thou hast given me: for thou lovedst me before the foundation of the world (John 17:24).

It is little wonder, then, that John assured us:

> Every man that hath this hope in him puri-
> fieth himself, even as he is pure (1 John 3:3).

Living in an earthly body subjects us to many irritations, but we will not live here forever. The hope of
sharing the life of God throughout eternity covers our
present afflictions with the limited presence and nature
of God that is now available to us. This hope forms a
pearl of beauty that may become part of a string of
pearls that could adorn the neck of our bridegroom
lover at the marriage supper of the Lamb.

As irritating as the body can sometimes be, it is but
the beginning of irritations for us. Early in our childhood, loving parents forced us to deal with the demands
of the soul or our human nature. Even David fought his
inner nature. He was convinced that dwelling in the
presence of God required a firm control over human
nature. He wrote:

> Who shall ascend into the hill of the Lord? or
> who shall stand in his holy place? He that
> hath clean hands, and a pure heart; who hath
> not lifted up his soul unto vanity, nor sworn
> deceitfully (Psalm 24:3-4).

This sounds so much easier than it practices, for
God's redemption does not remove our inner nature; it
merely renews it. Even this renewed nature can be irritating. As we shall see, it even irritated Jesus. O

CHAPTER THREE

THE IRRITATION OF HUMAN NATURE

IF THE LIMITATIONS of a human body irritated Jesus, how do you suppose He reacted to human nature? He, who had always been eternal God, defined His nature to Moses as:

> The Lord, The Lord God, merciful and gracious, longsuffering, and abundant in goodness and truth (Exodus 34:6).

Then He was born in a human body with the nature all mankind struggles to control. His problem was not so much one of self-control as it was of reacting to the nature of those with whom He dealt.

It has long been said that the only thing predictable about human nature is that it is unpredictable. This old proverb contains a measure of truth, but men and women who have studied human nature have given us some additional guidelines for understanding our natural tendencies. This includes a recognition that we have some inherent, basic drives. These include:

1. Self-preservation
2. Food seeking
3. Self-propagation
4. Possession
5. Dominion
6. Worship

Every sin known to humanity can be traced to the violation or perversion of one of these basic drives that God has put in our human nature. These drives are necessary for life, and they are pure until mishandled.

Self-preservation is the first law of life. We each have an instinctive urge to preserve ourselves. It is an ever-growing drive; we often call it *caution*. Even a baby possesses it and will throw out its arms when it feels itself falling. God addressed this in the Ten Commandments by declaring: "Thou shalt not kill" (Exodus 20:13). The need for self-preservation breeds hatred, fear and murder when it is allowed to become perverted.

Food seeking is actually the strongest drive in humanity, and it will sublimate all other drives if it is not satisfied. We will devote most of our strength and time to meeting this need until it is satisfied. Speaking from Mount Sinai, God said that food seeking must give place to worship. That is why He prohibited the Israelites from working on the seventh day (see Exodus 20:8-10). When this drive gets out of control, people turn to gluttony, smoking, drinking, drugs and Sabbath desecration.

The third strongest drive in human nature is *self-propagation*. Consciously or unconsciously, we humans are controlled by the mating instinct. This tremendously powerful law of nature is both God-given and God-ordained. We all want to reproduce ourselves through our children. The Ten Commandments addressed this drive in two ways: "Honor thy father and thy mother...Thou shalt not commit adultery" (Exodus 20:12,14). God demanded the preservation of the sanctity of the home and the purity of marriage. When our sex drive gets out of control, it produces adultery, fornication, divorce and sexual perversion.

The fourth human drive is the yearning for *possession*. Adam was told to possess Eden, and every "Adam" since then has had a longing to possess. Even babies strain and stretch to get their hands on something that looks interesting to them. The God-given law warned against letting this drive get out of control. God said: "Thou shalt not covet...." (Exodus 20:17). Out of control, this drive for possession breeds robbery, cheating, dishonesty and refusal to pay our tithe to the Lord.

The fifth natural drive is *dominion*. This is not something that has to be learned; it is inherent. Watch siblings fight to have dominion. They will eventually establish a chain of command among themselves. The law addresses this drive in saying: "Thou shalt not bear false witness against thy neighbor" (Exodus 20:16). This drive can be very damaging when it becomes out of control. It produces selfishness, abuse, pride and refusal to submit to God.

The sixth characteristic of human nature is *worship*. The issue is never *if* we will worship but rather *whom* we will worship, for worship is a basic instinct. The person does not exist who does not worship something or someone. On the mountain, God warned: "Thou shalt have no other gods before me" (Exodus 20:3). When this need is out of control, we worship idols — movie idols, pleasures, sex, things, money and even ourselves.

In their pure form these drives are the backbone of living, but when used impurely they are cancerous to human nature. It was the perversion of these drives in humanity (not their presence) that became very irritating to Jesus. Jesus Himself kept these drives in perfect control and used them to fulfill the Father's purposes for His life. He was sinless, so He found it difficult to understand how sin had so warped and corrupted these instincts in mankind.

The sin and selfishness and much of the sickness Jesus dealt with during His ministry on earth were the result of perverted human nature. He even faced this perversion in the men He chose to be His disciples. They became proud after a time of successful ministry. They fought among themselves for positions of prominence. Judas, at least, was greedy, and the rest of the disciples brought criticism upon Jesus for plucking grain on the Sabbath. How irritating it must have been to try to make disciples out of men whose human natures so dominated their thinking.

Our human nature becomes an obnoxious irritant to our spirits after we have been born again. Many Christians live most of their lives before they learn that these basic drives are good servants but miserable masters. Harmony reigns when human nature is a slave to the soul/spirit, but when the soul/spirit submits to the rule of our basic instincts, tyranny prevails. We have the option of living in the realm of our senses or in the realm of the spirit.

The principle of sensory domination of life is demonstrated all around us. Look at those who are controlled by physical appetites. They become compulsive eaters, drinkers or drug addicts. The cravings of the physical body control their every waking moment. They will steal and even kill in order to secure what the body craves. Careers, families and self-esteem are sacrificed just to meet the yearnings of the body.

The same thing is seen in people who are grossly

immoral. They have given in to their physical desires for sexual stimulation to such a degree that morality is sacrificed for gratification. The fact that this behavior destroys marriages, breaks up families and often stirs such anger as to threaten their lives is ignored in the indulgence of these lusts.

Appetite and sexual drives are normal to the human body. The most devout Christian experiences them. These drives are God-created, and He has provided proper channels for their expression and fulfillment. These and other physical desires are not sinful until they become controlling forces or are satisfied outside the limitations of God's provision.

The passions and lusts of our human nature can be irritating to our spirit. They prod, pry and goad us to actions and attitudes that are contrary to the will of God for our lives, and their ultimate goal is to be in charge. Paul put it this way:

> For the flesh lusteth against the Spirit, and the Spirit against the flesh: and these are contrary the one to the other: so that ye cannot do the things that ye would (Galatians 5:17).

All of us have experienced physical hunger sensations when we set aside a time to pray, or such fatigue overwhelms us that sleep seems to be an absolute necessity. Some Christians have jokingly said that the quickest answer to insomnia is to begin to pray!

Many Christians have been horrified to feel sexual desires rise when they worship God. These are merely attempts from within the realm of the soul to hinder the spirit from contacting God. These urges are effective only if we surrender to them. Peter warned of such attacks:

> Dearly beloved, I beseech you as strangers
> and pilgrims, abstain from fleshly lusts,
> which war against the soul (1 Peter 2:11).

He admitted the conflict, but he declared that fleshly desires can be handled. We can cover them with Christ's discipline so that they do not rule us, but we rule them. We can abstain from fulfilling them. There is a conflict, but we can be pearlmakers when we allow Christ's life to rule in us.

On some occasions in the Old Testament the Holy Spirit clothed Himself with human flesh, as in the case of Samson. Where the King James translation says, "The Spirit of the Lord came mightily upon him" (Judges 14:6,19; 15:14), the literal Hebrew says, "The Spirit of the Lord clothed Himself with Samson." It was God working though a human instrument, much as He did when speaking through the prophets. But Jesus did not simply borrow a human body — He became human.

Jesus understands the conflicts we endure in our souls because He was limited to the physical capacity of a healthy, adult Jewish male, and He was subject to the human nature that motivates, directs and controls the body. Jesus was plagued by basic drives and instincts common to human nature that sought to divert His attention from the divine mission He had come to fulfill.

We have a high priest who can be touched by the feeling of our infirmities and was in all points tempted as we are but was without sin (see Hebrews 4:15). That means Jesus not only grew weary, but He also had to contend with laziness and self-centeredness. He not only suffered hunger, but He had to contend with a hunger that was out of control. The potential for these and other excesses came with the human nature with which Jesus was born.

Our human nature can cause disaster when left uncontrolled. Paul warned the new Christians in Galatia:

> Now the works of the flesh are manifest, which are these; adultery, fornication, uncleanness, lasciviousness, idolatry, witchcraft, hatred, variance, emulations, wrath, strife, seditions, heresies, envyings, murders, drunkenness, revellings, and such like: of the which I tell you before, as I have also told you in time past, that they which do such things shall not inherit the kingdom of God (Galatians 5:19-21).

These sins are not the works of the devil but what the drives of human nature are capable of producing when allowed free, unbridled rein. Paul's answer to these out-of-control inner drives is:

> This I say then, Walk in the Spirit, and ye shall not fulfil the lust of the flesh...If we live in the Spirit, let us also walk in the Spirit (Galatians 5:16,25).

When we allow the Spirit of Christ to live in and through us, He will treat the irritation of our human nature as Jesus treated it. He will allow the living presence of the Holy Spirit to surround these carnal desires until they are no longer painful pressures in our lives. Then, instead of the disastrous works of the flesh, we will demonstrate the beautiful fruit of the Spirit.

> But the fruit of the Spirit is love, joy, peace, longsuffering, gentleness, goodness, faith, meekness, temperance: against such there is

> no law. And they that are Christ's have cruci-
> fied the flesh with the affections and lusts
> (Galatians 5:22-24).

None of this is automatic or instantaneous. Just as it takes gradual coverings of nacre to produce a pearl, it takes progressive coverings of the work of the Spirit to bring beauty to the irritating human nature with which we are born. We cannot successfully get away from our humanity, but we can bring it under the control of the Holy Spirit and make it a thing of beauty and utility for God's purposes. Paul suggests:

> For if ye live after the flesh, ye shall die: but
> if ye through the Spirit do mortify the deeds
> of the body, ye shall live...Mortify therefore
> your members which are upon the earth; for-
> nication, uncleanness, inordinate affection,
> evil concupiscence, and covetousness, which
> is idolatry (Romans 8:13; Colossians 3:5).

The New King James Version uses the phrase "put to death" in place of the word *mortify*. We cover these things with the indwelling life of the Holy Spirit much as we place a corpse in a casket. It is a deliberate action.

Jesus was plagued by His human nature, but He made a servant out of it. He didn't take the approach of an ascetic and deny these natural drives. By the power of the indwelling Holy Spirit He channeled these and made them serve the greater purpose of God.

This is the will of God for our lives. There is nothing immoral or improper with any basic human drive. God created us with all of them. We would starve to death without the drive of appetite. Without the sex drive, we probably would not reproduce. Those who lack the drive of possession do not save for the future. And if everyone did not have some drive for dominion, we would become the vassal slaves of anyone who claimed to be a leader.

The mere presence of these drives does not cause destruction. It is their distortion or corruption which produces the sins of the flesh. Food seeking, under control, is life giving, but food seeking that takes control of one's life can be disastrous.

Our society is very sense-oriented. In overemphasizing this we often become sensual, lustful and uncontrolled. Many people live under the dominion of physical appetites.

But we need not be filled with inordinate lusts and affections. God has provided that we can be filled with all the fullness of Himself. Just as God needed the humanity of Jesus to demonstrate His love, He needs our humanity in the world today. He does not desire that we deny our being, for "man...is the image and glory of God" (1 Corinthians 11:7), and "we should be to the praise of his glory" (Ephesians 1:12). Accordingly, then, God does not want us to denigrate or disparage our human nature. What He does desire is:

> That every one of you should know how to possess his vessel in sanctification and honor (1 Thessalonians 4:4).

God wants us to allow the Spirit of Christ to cover the lusts and desires of our basic nature until we produce a beautiful pearl, worthy to be worn around the neck of our Jesus at the marriage supper of the Lamb.

Of course, not everyone understood this disciplined and anointed nature of Jesus, but misunderstanding was another irritant that the Pearlmaker had to overcome. O

CHAPTER FOUR

THE IRRITATION OF MISUNDERSTANDING

GOD IS A GOOD communicator. The entire world in which we live was created in response to the commands of God. His instructions were comprehended clearly and carried out efficiently. He cried from eternity:

> Let there be light: and there was light. And God saw the light, that it was good: and God divided the light from the darkness (Genesis 1:3-4).

Adam seemed to have no difficulty understanding God, nor did Abraham or Moses. Even the children of Israel understood the voice of God as He thundered from Sinai:

> I am the Lord thy God, which have brought thee out of the land of Egypt, out of the house of bondage. Thou shalt have no other gods before me (Exodus 20:2-3).

The prophets were able to understand God, whether He spoke to them in a word, a vision or a dream. They faithfully told their generation the will of God.

It was to be expected, then, that when God came in human form He would be understood even more easily. After all, shouldn't a man be able to understand another man better than he can understand an unseen Spirit?

As life has proven to each of us, the obvious can sometimes be obscure. Jesus did not meet with consistent understanding. People even misunderstood His supernatural birth. For example, the wise men from the East comprehended the meaning of the star and followed it to Jerusalem where they explained their mission to King Herod. By researching the Old Testament Scriptures, the scribes confirmed the conclusions of these learned scholars, but Herod refused to believe either the scribes or the scholars. All he could envision was a future contender to his throne.

He immediately set wheels of destruction in motion, killing all the male children in the Bethlehem region who were three years old or less. Because Jesus' birth was so misunderstood by Herod, hundreds of innocent babies were slaughtered. With the advantage of hindsight this misunderstanding seems almost inconceivable, but it happened in the foreknowledge of God. The prophet Jeremiah had predicted it:

> Thus saith the Lord; A voice was heard in Ramah, lamentation, and bitter weeping; Ra[c]hel weeping for her children refused to be comforted for her children, because they were not (Jeremiah 31:15).

God expected to be misunderstood right from the beginning. He knows all too well how difficult it is for an evil heart of unbelief to accept divine truth. Prejudice, pride and personal ambition consistently blind people to the ways of God.

Human misunderstanding was a constant irritant to Jesus. When He was but a boy, He encountered it in his parents. They had taken Him to the temple for the yearly feast of the Passover, and He became so engrossed with the teaching of the scribes and religious rulers that He didn't realize His family had started home. Mary and Joseph discovered His absence the next day and returned to Jerusalem to search for Him.

> And it came to pass, that after three days they found him in the temple, sitting in the midst of the doctors, both hearing them, and asking them questions. And all that heard him were astonished at his understanding and answers. And when they saw him, they were amazed: and his mother said unto him, Son, why hast thou thus dealt with us? behold, thy father and I have sought thee sorrowing. And he said unto them, How is it that ye sought me? wist ye not that I must be about my Father's business? (Luke 2:46-49).

What He was doing seemed totally natural to Jesus. He found it difficult to understand why His parents were upset with Him. Was it possible that they did not understand His goals in life? Even as a boy Jesus sensed that He was to obtain higher goals than being a carpenter in Nazareth.

Although He quickly submitted and returned with them to Nazareth, an irritating grain of misunderstanding lodged in his inner being. He was just beginning to realize that He was different, but His parents didn't seem to share this recognition. Although it hurt, He didn't let it make Him rebellious.

When He matured to manhood, Jesus prepared Himself for ministry. The first miracle He performed didn't seem to be linked to who He was or why He had come. His mother asked Him to intervene when the wine supply was exhausted at a wedding celebration. He, the Savior of the world, was asked to salvage a bridegroom's pride by making up for the shortage. Jesus turned water into wine for the sake of His mother's wishes and His friend's needs.

His mother's acceptance of Him as a need-meeter proved to be the common recognition given to Him by the multitudes. As long as He healed their sick and fed their stomachs, the people would flock to Him, but when He taught the principles of the kingdom of God, they forsook Him. This misunderstanding of His mission on earth became so pronounced that Jesus rebuked those who only followed Him because He gave them bread (See John 6:26).

> Many of his disciples went back, and walked
> no more with him. Then said Jesus unto the
> twelve, Will ye also go away? (John 6:66-67).

Jesus did come to meet the needs of people, but it was painful to Him to find them so bound to their physical needs that they were unaware of the deeper need of their spirits. After teaching the multitude about God's provision for the lilies and the birds, He assured them:

> If then God so clothe the grass, which is to
> day in the field, and to morrow is cast into the
> oven; how much more will he clothe you, O
> ye of little faith? (Luke 12:28).

He was never unconcerned about the physical needs of others, but He was more concerned about the people's lack of interest in spiritual values. He followed the above encouragement with:

> For all these things do the nations of the world seek after: and your Father knoweth that ye have need of these things. But rather seek ye the kingdom of God; and all these things shall be added unto you (Luke 12:30-31).

Jesus did not want His mission to be interpreted as a one-man welfare program. He came as a revealer of the Father, but people preferred to view Him as their source of supply for physical wants. It hurt. It hurt deeply. It was an irritation that followed Him to the cross.

It seemed that misunderstanding plagued Jesus no matter what He said or did. Even His teaching ministry was misunderstood. He reduced His teaching to simple stories and parables, but even His handpicked disciples often missed the meaning of these. After listening to Jesus teach the parable of the sower:

> Then Jesus sent the multitude away, and went into the house: and his disciples came unto him, saying, Declare unto us the parable of the tares of the field (Matthew 13:36).

In spite of a year and a half of association with Jesus, they didn't comprehend His message. Earlier that day:

> The disciples came, and said unto him, Why speakest thou unto them in parables? He answered and said unto them, Because it is

> given unto you to know the mysteries of the
> kingdom of heaven, but to them it is not
> given (Matthew 13:10-11).

God had provided them with understanding hearts, but somehow they didn't know how to exercise this discernment. They enjoyed participating with Jesus in the miracles, but they consistently misunderstood even His simplest teaching. At least seven times Jesus clearly told His disciples about His impending death and resurrection, yet when it happened, they didn't understand. What an irritation this must have been to Jesus.

Did anyone understand Him? Herod misunderstood the purpose of His birth. His parents misunderstood His goals in life. The multitudes misunderstood His mission, and His own disciples did not understand His teaching.

It is to be expected, then, that His very existence would be misunderstood. Although He repeatedly spoke of who He was, people preferred to form their own opinions. Jesus asked His disciples:

> Whom do men say that I the Son of man am?
> And they said, Some say that thou art John
> the Baptist: some, Elias; and others, Jere-
> mias, or one of the prophets (Matthew 16:13-
> 14).

Like all religion that has followed since then, these people were unprepared or unwilling to accommodate a fresh revelation. They interpreted everything God was doing by past experiences. They found it easier to believe that a former prophet had risen from the dead than to accept Christ's statement that He was God who had come in the flesh. Hearing this report of what people were saying about Him, Jesus asked His disciples:

But whom say ye that I am? And Simon Peter
answered and said, Thou art the Christ, the
Son of the living God. And Jesus answered
and said unto him, Blessed art thou, Simon
Bar-jona: for flesh and blood hath not revealed it unto thee, but my Father which is in
heaven (Matthew 16:15-17).

What a breath of fresh air this must have been to the
soul of Jesus! Finally someone had accepted the revelation of the Father. He blessed Peter and said He would
build His church on this confession of faith. Yet within
three verses Peter rebuked Jesus for talking about the
cross. Jesus had this to say to Peter:

Get thee behind me, Satan: thou art an of-
fence unto me: for thou savourest not the
things that be of God, but those that be of
men (Matthew 16:23).

Dear foot-in-the-mouth Peter! He had received a
revelation of the person of Jesus, but he still misunderstood His mission and goals.

How did Jesus keep going? How did He handle this
consistent misunderstanding? He handled it in the same
manner that the oyster handles the grain of sand. If the
sand lodges in its soft flesh, the oyster forms a sac
around it to contain it. As time goes by, it continues to
pour layer after layer of nacre into the sac, which eventually forms a pearl.

Jesus kept this misunderstanding contained. He
didn't let it get to His spirit. While others misunderstood His birth, goals, mission, teaching and person, His
Father understood it perfectly. Jesus spent much time
talking this over with Him. It enabled Him to cover this

irritation with God's acceptance. This exuding of confidence of His relationship with the heavenly Father covered this irritation so completely that it did not become destructive to Jesus.

Christians also have seasons when they are grossly misunderstood. Their motives are questioned, their ministries are misunderstood and their mission in life is despised or compromised. It is irritating to give ourselves in ministry to others, only to meet with constant misunderstanding.

Sometimes our goals are misunderstood because of our mannerisms. Because we do not do things exactly as others would do them, we are misunderstood. Often the mere word patterns we use cause such misinterpretation. I have discovered that when I am preaching, a phrase may mean one thing to me and an entirely different thing to the ones listening to me. People have accused me of preaching wrong doctrine just because they applied my statements one way when I meant and applied them in another.

All of us want to be understood. It is irritating to be misunderstood, but it will happen. Jesus said:

> Verily, verily, I say unto you, The servant is not greater than his lord; neither he that is sent greater than he that sent him (John 13:16).

If the goals, mission and teaching of Jesus were misunderstood, it will happen to His servants, too.

I had a successful construction business in the same city where Judson was a pastor. When God brought him into the ministry and message of praise, I found him hard to understand. Although I was not a member of his church, I would visit there occasionally. When he led praise and worship, I found it very uncomfortable.

I was not alone in this. Our parents were members of his church; but this became too much for them, too, and they moved to another town. Our whole family took a position of "let's watch and see."

I watched Judson as people left his church because they couldn't understand his teaching on praise. I saw his denomination come down very heavily on him for several years. I became aware that members of his church board were seeking some occasion against him so he could be dismissed as pastor.

I wanted so much to help him, but he was convinced that God had commissioned him to bring praise to our area. My pastor criticized him from the pulpit, and other pastors withdrew from his fellowship. Our brother Robert served on the district presbytery and told me that Judson was often the subject of conversation in their meetings. They treated him like a hot potato.

Judson's church was building a larger sanctuary during all this misunderstanding. Somehow he was able to inspire the men to do the work and the women to assist them. His congregation continued to grow in spite of what others were saying about them. Instead of becoming overly defensive and bitter, his congregation manifested a gracious love to all who came among them, and my brother's sermons never seemed to lash out at those of us who couldn't, or wouldn't, see what he saw.

I would often stop by to see how the construction of the building was progressing, and I would find morning prayer meetings where praise and worship ascended up to God. I knew that my brother was giving himself more to prayer than ever before. Though he was acting as the contractor for the construction, he continued to go into God's presence for reassurance and guidance. Instead of exploiting the pain of misunderstanding, Judson and his congregation became pearlmakers.

The more Judson's congregation prayed, the more they appeared to be immune to what others were saying about them. Their ministry began to reach out to other congregations in the city and then throughout the state. After a season Judson's ministry began to reach up and down the West Coast, until God finally released him to the church at large.

I couldn't tell if my brother was so naive that he didn't realize how misunderstood and rejected he was or whether he had learned a way of handling this without letting it destroy him. Over the years I realized he had learned to let the life of Christ within him cover these irritating misunderstandings so that they didn't hurt him so much. But now it is evident that his confidence in his relationship with God brought forth a beauty that has blessed thousands of people who have attended his public ministry or read his books.

Now it is my joy to be Judson's pastor, for he works out of my church. Because I am now a participant in praise and worship, I understand how important and scriptural it is. Because I have seen how vital a contemporary relationship with God the Father is in handling the irritation of misunderstanding, I, too, have taught my congregation to praise, worship and pray privately and publicly. As I have brought my congregation into this response to God, we, too, have had to learn to handle misunderstanding.

Misunderstanding and accusations are tools used by both men and demons. Today's church seems to be filled with misunderstanding, which leads to accusations without proper grounds. If Jesus found security and relief in God's acceptance, we should be able to do the same. Does it matter whether or not we are understood by others as long as God understands our hearts?

If our motives are pure, then our rewards are secure, for God judges by the heart, not by the results.

None of us wants to suffer the pain of misunderstanding. But while we try to be understood, we need to prepare for the pain of misunderstanding. Anyone who has a fresh vision or revelation will be unappreciated. The church probably dislikes nothing more than change, yet God is in the business of changing us, and this always threatens us. When we see another person being changed, we would rather reject him or her than recognize that we could be next in line for change.

Perhaps it would help us if we would remember that this is nothing new. The Jews rejected Jesus because He didn't fit their religious mold. He made claims that were new, and He taught principles which they had overlooked, although these could be found in the Old Testament. He called for a discipline that was very unlike the sacrificial system they understood. Fortunately, Jesus did not let this misunderstanding hinder His true mission. He found relief from the pressure in the presence and acceptance of God the Father.

When faced with the rejection of misunderstanding, we need to let the life of the Pearlmaker in us form a protective sac around us while we liberally pour the nacre of our relationship with Father God into that sac — like Marvin the oyster did in covering his irritating piece of sand.

If we can learn to handle misunderstanding in a positive manner, it will help us resist temptation, for pleasing God will be far more important than pleasing others or ourselves. In the next chapter we will look at the way Jesus handled the irritation of temptation. O

CHAPTER FIVE

THE IRRITATION OF TEMPTATION

I HAVE UNDERGONE major surgery on my hands and shoulders. Yet I must admit that if I get a paper cut while opening an envelope, I fret over this minor wound more than I did over the surgeon's knife. The paper cut is not serious, but it is irritating. It seems that everything I touch reminds me of its presence. I catch myself saying what I've so often heard others say: "Nothing hurts like a paper cut." Intellectually I know this isn't so, but I'm emotionally irritated.

Temptation is a lot like a paper cut. It isn't serious, unless it leads us into sin, but it is annoying. It just doesn't seem to go away. Jesus experienced this aggravation when He was on the earth. Consider the circumstances that preceded one of Christ's severest temptations.

Before Jesus embarked on His ministry, He went to the Jordan River to be baptized by John. John pled his unworthiness, but Jesus insisted that He be allowed to fulfill all righteousness by being obedient in submitting to water baptism. In being our example as well as our Redeemer, Jesus had to be obedient in all things both great and small. As we read in Matthew 3:16-17:

> And Jesus, when he was baptized, went up straightway out of the water: and, lo, the heavens were opened unto him, and he saw the Spirit of God descending like a dove, and lighting upon him: And lo a voice from heaven, saying, This is my beloved Son, in whom I am well pleased.

Jesus was at least thirty years of age at this time — more likely thirty-three years old. He had never had an outside witness that He was the Son of God until this day. He'd had an awareness of being different from others since His childhood, but there was no external evidence of it. His mother had heard the prophecies in the temple at the circumcision of Jesus, but there is no indication in the Bible that she had ever shared them with her child. But when John saw Him, he cried:

> Behold the Lamb of God, which taketh away the sin of the world (John 1:29).

What a glorious day this must have been. Jesus' inner knowledge of who He was had finally been confirmed with outer signs. Jesus now had the testimony of three witnesses: John, the Spirit and the Father. He dared to believe that He was, indeed, the Son of God. The fact that He had three witnesses corresponds perfectly with this verse in 2 Corinthians:

> In the mouth of two or three witnesses shall

51

every word be established (2 Corinthians 13:1).

After such confirmation and fresh anointing, we might expect Jesus to be led into Jerusalem to launch His ministry, but instead we read:

> Then was Jesus led up of the Spirit into the wilderness to be tempted of the devil. And when he had fasted forty days and forty nights, he was afterward an hungered (Matthew 4:1-2).

He was to learn what most Christians have since discovered: all fresh experiences will be tested. He had to find out whether He had experienced an emotional level of excitement or whether God had actually proclaimed Him to be His Son.

This forty-day separation from other people and abstinence from food — likely a new experience for our Lord — weakened Jesus both physically and emotionally.

> And when the tempter came to him, he said, If thou be the Son of God, command that these stones be made bread (Matthew 4:3).

We've all learned that the devil tempts us when we are weak. Satan's first challenge to Jesus was: "If thou be the Son of God." The tempter hurled a challenge at Jesus' identity. It was not a challenge to anything He had done; it was a challenging denial of who He was.

This was neither Satan's first nor his last challenge to a believer's identity. In the Garden of Eden the serpent had hurled doubts to Eve in saying: "Hath God said?"

(Genesis 3:1). Satan still wants to create doubt in our lives in two major areas: (1) to doubt God's Word, and (2) to doubt God's work in making us His sons and daughters.

Jesus knew better than to accept Satan's challenge, and He knew that God never needs defending. But in spite of this knowledge, the temptation was irritating. Here the creature is daring to tempt the Creator to doubt who He is. It was as irritating as when a small child gives commanding orders to his or her mother. Jesus dared not doubt under pressure what had been declared to Him in public. How wisely we have been taught, "Never doubt in the darkness what you trusted in the light."

The "proof" Satan wanted was for Jesus to use His spiritual power for personal gain — "command that these stones be made bread" (Matthew 4:3). This would certainly have been convenient for Jesus, for He was hungry, but it would have been a misuse of His divine power. His ability to create food was illustrated twice when He multiplied bread and fish to feed the multitudes of people. Still, Jesus would not prostitute the power of Almighty God to meet His personal needs.

Neither should we. We do not need to prove we are Christians by coercing signs and wonders from God that are not in the will of God. Christ was fasting in God's will, and Satan tried to pull Him out of the will of God by tempting Him to justify His identity. Satan continues to use this ploy today. People try to produce miracles to show their anointing or giftings. Who we are in Christ does not depend upon the power we can display.

Satan also tempts people to use the power of the Holy Spirit to "make bread." All spiritual gifts have commercial value, and some people have become great merchandisers of spiritual abilities. They sell their ministry for a price; completely forgetting the command of Jesus:

> Heal the sick, cleanse the lepers, raise the
> dead, cast out devils: freely ye have received,
> freely give (Matthew 10:8).

The Holy Spirit comes as a certification of ministry, not as a commodity of merchandise. He is to be shared freely, not sold frugally. When we sell what belongs to another, it is thievery. Jesus resisted this temptation to misuse spiritual power even in the pain of a long fast. So should we.

When the first temptation did little more than irritate Jesus, Satan took a different approach.

> Then the devil taketh him up into the holy
> city, and setteth him on a pinnacle of the tem-
> ple, and saith unto him, If thou be the Son of
> God, cast thyself down: for it is written, He
> shall give his angels charge concerning thee:
> and in their hands they shall bear thee up, lest
> at any time thou dash thy foot against a stone
> (Matthew 4:5-6).

Having failed in trying to refute God's Word, Satan sought to use the Word for his own purposes. This was an accurate quote from Scripture but it was taken out of context.

Jesus knew what the devil was suggesting. Grandstanding spiritual power by jumping off this high pinnacle, Jesus would gather a great crowd and could then teach the principles of the kingdom. It appeared to be a way Jesus could gain acceptance with the people and fulfill His ministry at the same time. But Father God had a different way to draw people to Jesus, and His Son refused to deviate from it.

> Jesus said unto him, It is written again, Thou shalt not tempt the Lord thy God (Matthew 4:7).

In the past few years we've seen too many people calling attention to themselves with some spiritual gift or power. They have learned to grandstand God for their personal advantage and gain. They surrendered to the very temptation Jesus conquered. We Christians would do well to realize that anything which draws attention away from the Father to ourselves has the devil behind it in some way.

Jesus did not expand His ministry with hype and sensationalism. He remained faithful to the Word of God and proclaimed it with the power of God. Maybe members of the body of Christ should cease following the leaders who base their ministries on hype, exaggeration and sensationalism. It doesn't follow the pattern of Jesus — as a matter of fact, it seems to be a submission to the very temptation that Jesus resisted.

The third temptation Satan presented seems the most ludicrous of them all. He attempted to get Jesus to worship him. We read:

> Again, the devil taketh him up into an exceeding high mountain, and sheweth him all the kingdoms of the world, and the glory of them; And saith unto him, All these things will I give thee, if thou wilt fall down and worship me (Matthew 4:8-9).

Replacing God as the object of worship had been

Satan's goal in heaven, and in tempting Jesus to worship him he sought to fulfill it on earth. Satan's promise was to give Jesus everything He came to repossess in the first place. It was an offer to bypass the cross. To have bowed before Satan might have given Jesus whatever limited control Satan has wrested from men on this earth, but it would not have redeemed men and women back to God.

This was not the end of irritating temptations for Jesus. Dr. Luke says the devil left Him only "for a season" (see Luke 4:13). There was more temptation to come. If temptation were a once-in-a-lifetime experience, we might resist it better; but it brings continuous irritation into our lives. To have won the temptation today does not prevent the enemy from introducing another temptation tomorrow or the next week. Jesus said of His disciples:

> Ye are they which have continued with me in
> my temptations (Luke 22:28).

Jesus handled these temptations by turning attention to One greater than Himself — the Father — and what He had said in His Word. Jesus resisted every temptation with "It is written...." He refused to deviate from God's revealed plan. If God said it, that settled it for Jesus. This Word of God became the spiritual nacre He used to coat the irritation of temptations.

We Christians need to learn to handle temptation the way Jesus did. We will not be tempted when we are strong. Satan waits until we are exhausted, discouraged or needy in some way. Remember that He did not attack Jesus until He had been isolated and hungry for forty days. We need to realize that we lack the strength to resist successfully. We must learn to turn our temptations over to God, who is never weakened or exhausted.

When I was still in my teens, the Lord called me into the ministry. I entered Bible school with every intention of following God's call on my life, but a series of misunderstandings set circumstances in motion that deeply hurt and wounded me. About that time I discovered that I had a propensity for business. I did very well in car sales until the manager of a department store talked me into taking managerial training with the purpose of replacing him.

Following this training I moved to another city and became the manager of a men's clothing store. I later managed a new department store that opened in our area. God blessed me with both favor and ability, but I became bored.

I had a chance to work in a lumberyard and learned the trade quickly. When a small lumberyard became available, I purchased it and made a profitable business out of it. From this, I moved into construction and made more money than I had ever dreamed possible.

Again I became bored with it and moved to Phoenix, where I entered the land sales business. The timing was perfect, and my connections were valuable. I soon learned how to put business deals together very successfully. Those who know the "old" Jim Cornwall will testify that if I met a person with money, I soon devised ways to separate some of it from him or her.

I seemed to have the "Midas touch." Everything I touched turned to income. I belonged to all the right clubs, drove a different car every few months and lived in a very luxurious house. Anything I wanted was available to me, for money is power. I was a millionaire before I was thirty.

I never renounced my faith. I faithfully gave to the work of the Lord, and I continued to work in a church in whatever town I was operating. I often led the singing on Sunday morning, and I consistently taught a Sunday school class. However, the more I developed the land sales business, the more I was needed on Sunday, and little by little I traded my consecration to the Lord for my consecration to making money.

Then God intervened. I discovered that the "gifts and calling of God are without repentance" (Romans 11:29). Although I had not followed through with God's call on my life, God had not abandoned me or that purpose. In His mercy He began to pull the rug out from under me. He completely stripped me of everything I had, and I fled to Europe for a season of hiding. When I returned home, I even had to spend time in prison as God began the process of changing me, much as He did with Jacob.

Then, to my amazement, the Lord challenged me to enter the ministry. For a few years I worked as an assistant pastor, and then God asked me to return to Phoenix and start a new church. With great enthusiasm and with a confidence that it would be one of the easiest things I would ever do, I obeyed. Renting a school building, I put an ad in the paper and started my church with those who responded.

It didn't take me very long to realize that the old business principles I had developed would not work in God's business. God is not only anxious for His work to get done, but He is anxious that we do it by His principles. I found God's way slow, laborious and apparently unrewarding. We never had enough money for the things that needed to be done. My family and I lived in a small apartment, and we purchased a very run-down piece of property for our meeting hall. It was a totally different way of life for me.

During this time I faced constant temptations to use some of my old skills to "help God out." I was tempted to get back into land sales, but after selling a few houses for a realtor, I recognized that it conflicted with my calling to the ministry.

Once I purchased a building to be moved onto our property and joined to the small existing building. I was tempted to use some of my old skills to transfer money from the rich to "help the poor," but God helped me to realize that this was but a temptation to return to an old way of life.

Our congregational growth forced me to do another enlargement, and then we purchased the house next door and remodeled it into offices. My old flare for building came to light, and people marvelled at my skills in remodeling. Before long, different ones began to use me as a consultant in remodeling and decorating. It was almost as natural as eating, but it wasn't God's will for me anymore.

I will never cease to be amazed at how many different ways the devil can tempt us to turn from the calling of God and back to the convenience of our former ways. Years of praying and serving God have not totally removed old ambitions and desires upon which the enemy pulls. It is a continual source of irritation to me. I have learned, however, that the more I try to meet these temptations with willpower and resolve, the stronger they pull on me.

It is not the strength of Jim Cornwall that successfully resists the tempter. I have learned that I am no match for the tempter, but God's Word assures me:

> Ye are of God, little children, and have overcome them: because greater is he that is in you, than he that is in the world (1 John 4:4).

I have learned to lean on the strength of the written

Word of God as quickened to me by the Holy Spirit to resist the enemy's temptation successfully and to build a protective wall around the irritation of that temptation. God's promise is still very true:

> There hath no temptation taken you but such as is common to man: but God is faithful, who will not suffer you to be tempted above that ye are able; but will with the temptation also make a way to escape, that ye may be able to bear it (1 Corinthians 10:13).

Sometimes I regret having ever been in business. Perhaps I wouldn't face so many temptations if I didn't know how to make money. Then I read:

> Beloved, think it not strange concerning the fiery trial which is to try you, as though some strange thing happened unto you: But rejoice, inasmuch as ye are partakers of Christ's sufferings; that, when his glory shall be revealed, ye may be glad also with exceeding joy (1 Peter 4:12-13).

Jesus was tempted in all points as we are, but without sin (see Hebrews 4:15). The temptation is not sin; yielding to it is the sin. As long as we yield to the indwelling Holy Spirit, we will not submit to the temptation to take things into our own hands. I have also discovered that every time I let God handle the temptation, I become stronger and eventually Satan leaves me alone in that area of my life. Since he only attacks our weak areas, we need to become strong in the areas he has attacked in the past. And we can gain strength against Satan by remembering this promise:

> God is our refuge and strength, a very present
> help in trouble (Psalm 46:1).

We can also take comfort in knowing that Satan will
be defeated in the end:

> And I heard a loud voice saying in heaven,
> Now is come salvation, and strength, and the
> kingdom of our God, and the power of his
> Christ: for the accuser of our brethren is cast
> down, which accused them before our God
> day and night (Revelation 12:10).

No matter what the source of our temptation may be
— satanic, saints or self — it is irritating to our spiritual
lives, just as it was irritating to the life of Jesus. We
need to learn again the lesson we saw in Marvin the
oyster who used nacre to make a pearl out of irritating
sand. If we will just coat the irritation of temptation
with the settled Word of God, it will be covered with
layer after layer of spiritual nacre until an iridescent
pearl is formed that we may present to Jesus at His
coming.

The answer to temptation is not rigidity — it is relationship. The closer we walk with the living Word of
God as revealed in the written Word of God, the less
likely we are to fall into temptation or to embrace legalism as our defense against Satan. In the next chapter we
will look at how legalism among religious leaders came
in conflict with Jesus' ministry. O

CHAPTER SIX

THE IRRITATION OF LEGALISM

THERE HAS NEVER BEEN a day like it before or since. A vast throng of people that may have numbered in excess of two million stood on the desert floor at the foot of Mount Sinai. The mountain itself was ablaze with fire and covered with smoke. A loud, long trumpet blast brought the multitude to complete silence. Then the audible voice of God thundered out the Ten Commandments (see Exodus 20).

These were to become the fundamental principles that would guide Israel in their transition from slavery to becoming a nation under God. The Ten Commandments covered the fundamentals of relating to God, to one another and to oneself. This code is so simple and so practical that it became the foundation for English law, which in turn provided the basis for American law.

The Scriptures clearly show that this law was a direct communication from God to mankind. Therefore, when God was on earth in the form of Jesus, there would be nothing about that law that was disturbing to Him. Jesus even attested:

> Think not that I am come to destroy the law,
> or the prophets: I am not come to destroy, but
> to fulfill (Matthew 5:17).

It was not the law but legalism that became so irritating to Jesus. Don't bother to go to your concordance to look up *legalism*, for it is not a Bible word. You won't even find it in a Bible dictionary; neither Judson nor I could find it in the fifteen volumes of Bible dictionaries in our personal libraries. You will, however, find the word defined in a standard dictionary. Merriam-Webster's Seventh New Collegiate Dictionary defines legalism as: "strict, literal, or excessive conformity to the law or to a religious or moral code." The key word is *excessive*.

The Ten Commandments were as applicable in the days of Jesus as they were in the days of Moses. During the long span of years between Moses and Jesus, these God-given laws had been studied, analyzed, taught and enlarged. Scholarly rabbis had written personal commentaries on these laws that became as binding to the observers of Judaism as the actual commandments were. These writings had taken on the force of the law. By the time of Jesus, the Ten Commandments had been enlarged to more than two thousand laws, rules, regulations and requirements. The Talmud and the Targum, which contained many of these writings, were more fervently taught and rigidly enforced than were the commandments of God. This is a clear case of putting the words of men higher than the words of God. Jesus charged the religious rulers of His day with:

> Making the word of God of none effect
> through your tradition, which ye have deliv-
> ered: and many such like things do ye (Mark
> 7:13).

Few things irritated Jesus more than seeing man's rules and interpretations replace the clear command of God. These rules often overlooked the higher law of love and, frequently, made very little common sense. For example, when Jesus' disciples plucked a few heads of wheat and rubbed the chaff off in their hands to produce clean grains to eat, the Pharisees charged them with unlawful activity because it was the Sabbath day (see Matthew 12:1-2). The law did prohibit working on the Sabbath, but it was ridiculous to say that taking the husks off a few heads of wheat was equal to a threshing operation.

Legalism attempts to control by law and rules. The higher purposes of God are ignored if they seem to break one of the religious rules. The legalist seldom shows compassion. He or she overlooks the fact that the law was based on divine love. When Jesus was asked by a scribe what was the greatest commandment, He replied:

> Thou shalt love the Lord thy God with all thy
> heart, and with all thy soul, and with all thy
> mind. This is the first and great command-
> ment. And the second is like unto it, Thou
> shalt love thy neighbor as thyself. On these
> two commandments hang all the law and the
> prophets (Matthew 22:37-40).

To Jesus, the letter of the law was far less important than the spirit of the law, which is love. Paul picked up this concept in declaring that no amount of ministry or operation of the gifts of the Holy Spirit is profitable unless it flows in the channel of love (see 1 Corinthians 13).

On repeated occasions Jesus lovingly reached out to heal afflicted people on the Sabbath day, only to be questioned, rebuked and rebuffed by the purveyors of legalism and their followers.

In Matthew, immediately following the incident of eating the heads of wheat in the field on the Sabbath day, we read:

> And, behold, there was a man which had his hand withered. And they asked him, saying, Is it lawful to heal on the sabbath days? that they might accuse him (Matthew 12:10).

It was an obvious setup to pit Christ's compassion against their legalistic interpretation of the law of Moses. The poor man with the withered hand was merely a pawn in their game. They could not have cared less what happened to him, but Jesus cared.

> And he said unto them, What man shall there be among you, that shall have one sheep, and if it fall into a pit on the sabbath day, will he not lay hold on it, and lift it out? How much then is a man better than a sheep? Wherefore it is lawful to do well on the sabbath days. Then saith he to the man, Stretch forth thine hand. And he stretched it forth; and it was restored whole, like as the other (Matthew 12:11-13).

These men may have conformed to the letter of the

law, but they lacked the compassion of God in their hearts. Furthermore, they did not realize how little work was required to heal this hand. A word from Jesus and an obedient action by the man accomplished a creative miracle. Instead of the Pharisees rejoicing in the compassion and power of God, we read:

> Then the Pharisees went out, and held a council against him, how they might destroy him. But when Jesus knew it, he withdrew himself from thence: and great multitudes followed him, and he healed them all (Matthew 12:14-15).

Jesus met this same lack of compassion when He healed the lame man at the pool of Bethesda. After hearing the man's complaints about losing his turn to get into the water when an angel stirred it, Jesus said to him:

> Rise, take up thy bed, and walk. And immediately the man was made whole, and took up his bed, and walked: and on the same day was the sabbath (John 5:8-9).

For thirty-eight years this man had lain at the side of the pool hoping against hope that he would get healed. Jesus had compassion on him and healed only him that day. But the Jews would not rejoice at such a miracle:

> The Jews therefore said unto him that was cured, It is the sabbath day: it is not lawful for thee to carry thy bed. He answered them, He that made me whole, the same said unto me, Take up thy bed, and walk (John 5:10-11).

The Jews took immediate action when they discovered that this cure was the work of Jesus:

> Therefore did the Jews persecute Jesus, and
> sought to slay him, because he had done
> these things on the sabbath day (John 5:16).

The Bible says plainly that it was "the Jews" who complained. It was not only religious leaders who were distressed at the compassion of Jesus if its expression violated their teaching about the law. The very people who witnessed the miracles complained that they were done on the wrong day, in a wrong manner or to an unacceptable person. They had become so conditioned to what they thought was right and wrong that there was no room for compassion in their hearts. This is true of all legalists; strict observance of their interpretation of the rules supersedes everything else. This constantly annoyed Jesus, but He covered it by doing the will of His Father in spite of their anger.

I recently shared fellowship with a preacher who had such unconditional love for others that it naturally brought growth to his church. He received people from other denominations into membership by recognizing the baptism they had already experienced instead of demanding that they be rebaptized. Although the church had the highest attendance of its history, two charter members secured the services of a lawyer, who pointed out that according to their bylaws all such memberships were illegal because those baptisms were "foreign." By disenfranchising 90 percent of the congregation from voting privileges, 5 percent were able to vote the pastor out of office. Their "law of baptism" was more important than growth, conversions or spiritual enlargement. No wonder legalism angered Jesus.

People have often been "frozen out" of a church because members did not approve of their hairstyle, their dress code or the type of music to which they responded. It is often the case that these churches have great concern for lost souls on the mission field, but they cannot open their hearts to the hurting souls who dare to enter their churches. The observance of their codes is more important than the redemption of lost men and women.

The Gospel of Matthew shows repeatedly how legalistic the Pharisees were; remember that not all Pharisees were religious rulers. This was a sect of Judaism much as our denominations are branches of Christianity. Matthew records on one occasion:

> The Pharisees also came unto him, tempting him, and saying unto him, Is it lawful for a man to put away his wife for every cause? (Matthew 19:3).

They argued on the divorce issue and were not the least bit concerned with those who were divorced. They merely wanted to trap Jesus in this point of their law. They had seen His mercy extended to the woman caught in the very act of adultery, and they assumed that Jesus would violate the law in order to rescue someone. They could not realize that Jesus did not need to violate divine law to reach afflicted and hurting people, but He did have to step over the fences that legalism had erected. He still has to do this, for men make restrictions more formidable than God Himself does. Jesus had already told them:

> But if ye had known what this meaneth, I will have mercy, and not sacrifice, ye would not

have condemned the guiltless (Matthew 12:7).

Still, their biased minds could not conceive of mercy prevailing over the law. Religion rarely does, and this irritates Jesus.

Jesus, the Pearlmaker, let the spiritual nacre of common sense, compassion and mercy cover the irritation of legalism in others.

The more I pastor, the more irritated I become with legalism in the church. I am convinced that extreme legalism has kept more people away from Christ Jesus than sin and the devil combined. It seems that every fresh visitation of God to His people is followed by rigid application of law that degenerates into legalism.

This often begins quite innocently, for new converts want to know how to live righteously in Christ Jesus. Instead of repeatedly directing them to the righteous Christ, religion seeks to reduce the Christian life to a code of ethics and rules. Religion says that obedient observation of these laws guarantees a victorious Christian life. We embrace the erroneous concept that righteousness can be achieved by works and observation of rules. The Bible teaches that righteousness comes out of a relationship with God.

You may have experienced exactly what I am describing. Because of past teachings, you may be struggling through religious activities, attempting to be holy in God's sight. You may be obeying the letter of the law but not the spirit of God's law. Or you may have been needlessly hurt by legalism instead of helped by God's love extended through fellow Christians.

Six years ago I founded a new church that has known consistent growth. This ministry has required me to do much counseling, for it is usually troubled and hurt people who come to a new church. I have ached inwardly as I have listened to the stories of people who have almost been destroyed by religious codes and rules. Church members who have gone through a divorce have become some of my most active workers. Their former religious associates severely penalized even the victims or innocent parties of these divorces. These churches had moved their divorced members out of office or ministry and made them function as second-rate citizens. Their tithes were welcome, but nothing else about them was acceptable.

I do not wholeheartedly support divorce. I earnestly support strong marriages and families. I believe that divorce is sin, but it is not the unpardonable sin. God hates divorce, but He loves the ones who have been divorced just as much as He loves everyone else. All sin can be cleansed by the blood of Jesus Christ, and a new beginning is made available. Mercifully God's Word declares:

> Therefore if any man be in Christ, he is a new creature: old things are passed away; behold, all things are become new (2 Corinthians 5:17).

Either this is true or it is false. Where does it say "except divorced persons"? The hypocrisy of the adamant stand against divorce taken by some religious zealots irritates me. Perhaps they think that building high fences will prevent divorce, but those very same fences also prevent the rescuing of those who have been deeply wounded by divorce — which is about half the adult population in the United States.

These legalistic people have great compassion on murderers, drug addicts and homosexuals. They make public boasts whenever they restore such a person to a life in Christ. Nothing in the church is withheld from them. But this same compassion is withheld from anyone who has gone through divorce. I have to let the grace of God override the rules of men in order to let this irritation form a pearl within me instead of wounding me severely.

Because I spent so much time in the business world before entering the ministry, I can understand the unbeliever's expressed disgust with moral failures in Christian leaders. I do not understand these same emotions in believers in the body of Christ. What has happened to Christ's compassion? Where is Christian love? What has happened to the ministry of restoration? We need to return to the compassionate, loving message of Jesus:

> Neither do I condemn thee: go, and sin no more (John 8:11).

Since becoming a pastor, I have reached out to those who have experienced moral failure — both leaders and followers. Any legalist can condemn them; but with proper guidance and liberal application of Christ's love, these sinning saints can be restored to a vital ministry. The attitude of surprise I find in the people I have reached out to in mercy hurts me far more than the sin I hear them confess. They are amazed that anyone cares and are equally astonished that the Bible does not make ' this the end of the road for them.

Legalists claim that "the bird with the broken wing never flies as high again," but they must be ignoring Paul the murderer, David the adulterer and Peter, who cursed and swore as he denied Christ. These men rose to greater heights after divine restoration than they had achieved before they committed such gross sins.

71

The Bible never whitewashes sin, in spite of some evangelistic misapplications of Isaiah:

> Come now, and let us reason together, saith the Lord: though your sins be as scarlet, they shall be as white as snow; though they be red like crimson, they shall be as wool (Isaiah 1:18).

God does more than figuratively change the color of our sin — He removes it. Elimination — not alteration — is the way God handles sin. The promise of the New Testament is:

> If we confess our sins, he is faithful and just to forgive us our sins, and to cleanse us from all unrighteousness (1 John 1:9).

Jesus not only forgives confessed sin, He cleanses it from one's life. Heaven's records no longer list these sins, leaving us in a state of just-as-if-I'd-never-sinned (being *justified*).

For the legalists this seems too generous on God's part. They feel that some ongoing penalty needs to be imposed. In trying to be God's little helpers, they become major hindrances to the restoration of people who have sinned. This irritates me; but because I have received tremendous grace and mercy from the hand of Jesus, I can extend it to others and use some of it to cover the irritant of legalism.

Legalism is what infected the charismatic movement of the 1970s and gradually altered it. The beautiful love relationship between Christians and the Holy Spirit was quickly absorbed into various forms of discipleship training where rules replaced relationship, and human enforcement of those rules superseded walking in the Spirit.

In our human frailty we feel compelled to cry out, What must I do? rather than accept what Christ has done. None of us wants to be saved by grace plus nothing. We all feel convinced that there must be something we can do to enhance that salvation or help God effect that deliverance in our lives. In response to this innate cry, religious people develop codes of conduct that they often enforce more unyieldingly than the Word of God.

You may have experienced this when you came to Christ for salvation. Before you could fully appreciate the joy of your salvation, you may have been counseled immediately about the new rules by which you would have to live. You came in burdened with sin and left burdened with religion. Perhaps you couldn't tell much difference in the loads. These people may have meant well, but they were legalists who were quickly imposing upon you the limits they had set for themselves. Perhaps they had become so miserable in their search for righteousness by works that they could not tolerate your newfound joy in Jesus.

Extreme legalists seek to make every issue in life a spiritual issue. In the days of Jesus they tried to make a spiritual issue of paying taxes. We read:

> And when they were come, they say unto him, Master, we know that thou art true, and carest for no man: for thou regardest not the person of men, but teachest the way of God in truth: Is it lawful to give tribute to Caesar, or not? Shall we give, or shall we not give? But he, knowing their hypocrisy, said unto them, Why tempt ye me? bring me a penny, that I may see it. And they brought it. And he

> saith unto them, Whose is this image and su-
> perscription? And they said unto him, Cae-
> sar's. And Jesus answering said unto them,
> Render to Caesar the things that are Caesar's,
> and to God the things that are God's. And
> they marvelled at him (Mark 12:14-17).

Social and governmental obligations are not spiritual issues unless they seriously violate the clear, written commands of God. Because of my Pentecostal background I can understand why people make counseling appointments with me to discuss a dress code, whether they should attend the movies occasionally or if it is all right to take a vacation. The thing that irritates me is that legalists have made a spiritual issue out of such decisions. Does accepting Jesus as our Savior numb our minds into inactivity? God doesn't care if you wear a red tie or a blue one, and I don't believe God cares what kind of car you drive, as long as you can honestly afford it. I even believe that the choice of a lifetime mate is ours — subject to God's veto.

It is sad that the same Christians who declare that Jesus alone can save a person from sin feel that this saved person is then able to keep himself or herself in righteousness. Saving grace must be continually received. Jesus said:

> The thief cometh not, but for to steal, and to
> kill, and to destroy: I am come that they
> might have life, and that they might have it
> more abundantly (John 10:10).

Life — not legalism — is Christ's gift to the penitent one. Jesus came to bring joy back into living. His life is a life of peace and purpose. Christian conduct in the redeemed man or woman is maintained by submitting to Christ, not by struggling with rules.

Perhaps we need to look again at Marvin the oyster. When an outside irritation enters his shell, he contains it in a sack and pours nacre into it until that irritant is covered repeatedly. Eventually this produces a pearl. Our best answer to legalism's irritation is to cover it thoroughly with the written Word of God as the Holy Spirit makes it a living word in our hearts. Through this process the Holy Spirit can lead us in paths of righteousness. David was convinced that he did not need to follow a road map to walk in paths of righteousness. He wrote:

> He restoreth my soul: he leadeth me in the paths of righteousness for his name's sake (Psalm 23:3).

Following God's Spirit as He reveals God's Word will not only make our lives more beautiful and beneficial, but this irritant of legalism will become the seed of a pearl that is formed by the nacre of God's grace, mercy and compassion.

Following this route will, of course, open you to slander. When the legalists of Christ's day could not force Him into their religious mold, they openly slandered Him to discredit His ministry. Have you ever been slandered unjustly? Chapter 7 will show you how Jesus handled vicious, slanderous attacks from others. O

CHAPTER SEVEN

THE IRRITATION OF
SLANDER

LIKE AN INTERCONTINENTAL ballistic missile, slander is a dangerous and powerful weapon. It often destroys its victim before he or she can prepare a defense. Jesus suffered the pain of slanderous attacks by the religious leaders of His day.

Those of us whose lives have been transformed by the saving grace of Jesus have a hard time understanding the treatment He received at the hands of these religious leaders. We view Jesus as a Redeemer; they saw Him as a radical. To us Jesus is a friend, but they chose to make Him their enemy. They did not deny the good that He did, but they detested the way He did it, where He did it and when He did it. Their greatest problem with Jesus was that He operated outside the established religious system.

Wherever there are positions of authority, there will be power politics to fill those offices and to protect those who fill them. All religious systems have these authoritative positions and therefore have politics integrated into the system. During the days of Jesus, the power and politics of the Jewish religious structure were particularly forceful. The Roman government even provided the high priest with a unit of soldiers that functioned as his personal army.

That Jesus could be a threat to these entrenched leaders may seem curious, for He was far outside their ranks. He was neither born to the priesthood nor trained as a rabbi. He was just the son of Joseph — a carpenter from Nazareth. No one on the Sanhedrin was aware of anything in His background that would distinguish Him, but multitudes of people followed Him. His teachings were being repeated all over Israel. True politicians know how valueless an office becomes when the people turn to another leader.

While the religious authorities had the power and positions, Jesus had the people in the palms of His hands. To maintain their control, these leaders had either to discredit Jesus or destroy Him. This is the heartbeat of a political system — protect yourself no matter what it does to your opponent. The issue was never what was right or wrong. It was survival of the system, and Jesus threatened the religious status quo, so He was expendable.

During my years in the business world, whenever I sat as chairman of the board during corporate business meetings, I often had to lead the discussion about our competition. No matter how good our sales staff was or how acceptable our product had become, we had to be alert to our competitors. Always our first approach was to be better than they were.

When it seemed impractical or even impossible to beat them at their service or their product, we would attempt a buyout, especially if the competitor was a small, new company. When all else failed, we usually tried to discredit our opposition. By using advertising that asked leading questions, we were able to put doubt in the minds of potential buyers. These questions always projected the superiority of our company while suggesting the inferiority of the competition.

As I read my New Testament, I can almost imagine that I am attending a board meeting of the Sanhedrin as they discuss the problem of the Jesus competition:

Caiaphas, the high priest, opens the meeting with a warning. "After listening to testimonies extolling the miracles that Jesus performed, obviously we cannot match His performance. Furthermore, the figures on His growing popularity are alarming. If this rate continues for even a few years, our Sanhedrin will be out of business completely."

One of the lawyers present responds skeptically: "There is no option of a buyout, for Jesus doesn't even have an organization, just twelve unlearned disciples who follow Him everywhere. Furthermore, Jesus doesn't seem interested in a profit. How can you buy out a person who never sees money as part of His motivation?"

"Discredit Him!" someone shouts.

"But how?" the high priest asks. "We've sent our best lawyers and scribes to discredit Him with trick questions, but He consistently turns those questions to His advantage and disgraces our agents. When we tried to catch Him concerning paying tribute to Rome, He caused the multitude to roar with laughter with His answer. He just looked at a Roman tax coin and said, 'Render therefore unto Caesar the things which be Caesar's, and unto God the things which be God's' [Luke 20:25]. He has an uncanny ability to make the best of any situation we set up."

"Two of our best interrogators returned last week

with the report, 'Never man spake like this man' [John 7:46]," a scribe volunteers.

"I understand that after Nicodemus questioned Jesus, he became one of His disciples," cries another. "We can't afford any further defection."

"Let's go after His reputation then," the chief scribe suggests.

"Do you mean *slander* Him?" the high priest asks. "Does our law allow us to do that?"

After a short consultation among the lawyers, their spokesman responds conspiratorially, "A strict interpretation of the law would prohibit this, but sometimes the end justifies the means."

He certainly had precedent for this answer. He needed only to remember that Queen Jezebel had used this kind of rationalizing against Naboth the Jezreelite to secure his vineyard when he refused to sell it to King Ahab, who wanted it for a garden of herbs. She hired men to declare that Naboth had blasphemed God, so the elders stoned him. The irony of this is that this queen worshipped Baal and had killed many of God's prophets. The means was neither honest nor lawful, but Queen Jezebel felt that the end result of satisfying her husband's desire justified the slander of a commoner.

"This Jesus is the greatest threat to the law and our entire religious system that we've encountered in our lifetime. We'll do whatever we have to do. It's either slander or slaughter. If we can't discredit Him, we'll have to destroy Him," Caiaphas says.

"Then slander Him," the council agrees. "Assign some of our most informed lawyers and scribes to follow Jesus constantly. They need to watch for every chance to slander Him so effectively that the people will turn from following Him."

Perhaps I have an overactive imagination, but the

biblical account affirms that this was their plan:

> And as he said these things unto them, the
> scribes and the Pharisees began to urge him
> vehemently, and to provoke him to speak of
> many things: Laying wait for him, and seek-
> ing to catch something out of his mouth, that
> they might accuse him (Luke 11:53-54).

What an irritation this must have been to Jesus. He
knew what was in their hearts. He told the lawyers:

> Woe unto you, lawyers! for ye have taken
> away the key of knowledge: ye entered not in
> yourselves, and them that were entering in ye
> hindered (Luke 11:52).

From that point on, slander was more than an assign-
ment to the religious leaders. It had become their personal vendetta. Perhaps they made their most
devastating accusation after Christ delivered a blind
mute from the work of demons and thereby restored his
sight and ability to speak. Matthew records the incident:

> Then was brought unto him one possessed
> with a devil, blind, and dumb: and he healed
> him, insomuch that the blind and dumb both
> spake and saw. And all the people were
> amazed, and said, Is not this the son of
> David? But when the Pharisees heard it, they
> said, This fellow doth not cast out devils, but
> by Beelzebub the prince of the devils (Mat-
> thew 12:22-24).

They could not deny the miracle. However, these religious leaders saw an opportunity to discredit the source of power that produced the miracle, because the people themselves were so amazed that they were questioning the source of Jesus' power. The Pharisees sought to make Jesus an agent of Satan rather than recognize Him as the Son of God.

Jesus did not lash out in anger. Instead He answered them straightforwardly:

> And Jesus knew their thoughts, and said unto them, Every kingdom divided against itself is brought to desolation; and every city or house divided against itself shall not stand: And if Satan cast out Satan, he is divided against himself; how shall then his kingdom stand? And if I by Beelzebub cast out devils, by whom do your children cast them out? therefore they shall be your judges. But if I cast out devils by the Spirit of God, then the kingdom of God is come unto you (Matthew 12:25-28).

Jesus spoke words of truth, but the words of slander had been spoken first, making Christ's reply sound defensive to those who were listening. The success of malicious slander is to plant doubt in the minds of those who hear it so that even the truth will not completely dislodge it.

It is untrue to say that the slander of these religious rulers failed, for it produced doubt in enough minds that when it was time to crucify Jesus, vast multitudes cried, "Crucify Him! Crucify Him!" Slander is a deadly poison.

Although Christ's answer did not remove all the poison of the slander, it did cover that slander with such righteousness that it could have formed a pearl immense enough to be a gate in the New Jerusalem. The slander hurt, but that irritant ultimately produced something beautiful.

Religion still uses slander as a major weapon against nonconformists. I remember when Jack and Jane (not their real names) first came into my study. They had visited our church the preceding Sunday and asked for a time to talk with me. For six or seven years they had been faithful workers in a church in another community. They watched the pastor exert stronger and stronger control over the lives of the congregation until it bordered on cultic control. The preaching centered on the authority of the pastor and the duty of the people to support and follow him unquestioningly.

When this became intolerable for Jack and Jane, they made an appointment with the pastor to discuss this with him. As might be expected, the pastor condemned them severely for daring to question him in any way. He told them that they should repent before the congregation. When they said they would no longer attend that church, the pastor warned that if they left, they would forfeit their salvation and be lost eternally. This pastor condemned the two of them from the pulpit for the next few weeks and called them agents of the devil, warning the congregation to have nothing to do with them. He promised that those who continued to fellowship with them would be expelled from the church and condemned to the same damnation.

For months this couple lived in a state of shock. They had never expected such slanderous action. They had gone to their pastor directly instead of talking about him behind his back. Their only "sin" was in voting against his leadership by walking away. The slander that was spoken of them left them isolated from their former friends and associates. The severity and the success of the slander caused them to doubt their very salvation.

They were vacationing in our area when they saw our church sign and dared to come in for our Sunday service. They had not attended church for months, and this was an act of desperation.

In the mercy of God, they received a ray of hope through the love that was extended to them.

As I helped them understand that they had been wounded almost to death by slander, and that slander is false, they began to find their way out of their spiritual depression and despair. Their love and zeal for God have become an inspiration to others in our congregation now that they have moved to our area permanently. They have learned that while the damage that slander causes can seldom be undone in the lives of others who hear it, it need not destroy the lives of those against whom it was directed. They can cover it with the righteousness and acceptance of God and become pearlmakers.

Not too long ago I had an opportunity to counsel with a young pastor who, in some ways, reminded me of myself. He was a nonconformist, even in his Bible school days, but nonconformists are often good leadership material. They simply march to the beat of a different drummer. Feeling that he was called of God, he had gone into a bedroom district of a major city and started a church under the banner of his denomination.

The way he was doing things irritated his denominational leaders. The fact that he was succeeding by using his methods didn't seem to count. They wanted things done their way. His heavy emphasis on praise and worship disturbed them. After several years of conflict with them, he turned in his papers and informed his officials that he would start over as an independent minister.

They made him turn over all the equipment he had gathered and all money he had in the bank under the church name, and they informed him that the denomination would keep the congregation. Without malice or even an argument, this young pastor agreed to all their conditions.

His small congregation was aware of the struggle, so when he announced his resignation, they simply moved from the rented theater to the newly rented school auditorium and started over. Although God has obviously blessed both this pastor and his people, I found him deeply wounded by the slanderous announcement that was made in pulpits in the area: "Stay away from pastor so-and-so and his congregation. They have become New Agers."

This term had never been used in the three years of dialogue between him and his denomination. The issue of "wrong doctrine" had never been raised. Their disagreement had always been over his method of worship.

"How could they say such a thing about me?" was his question.

"Remember, brother," I told him, "slander is a false charge. Since they could find nothing truthful that would discredit you, they had to resort to slander. I thank God that you and your wife lived in the righteousness of Christ so that they lacked gossip to throw at you."

"What can I do to reverse the slander in the community?" he asked me.

"Probably nothing," I admitted. "Some people will believe the slander to their dying day because they deeply trust the person who spoke it. You can only learn to overcome the hurt of the slander in your personal life, and continue to live in such a way that the honest enquirer will be convinced that the slander is a lie."

Many newly saved wives have suffered severe slander from their unbelieving husbands. The change in life-style in one woman I counseled angered her husband, and his offensive weapon was false accusation and slander. He maligned her character, denied the reality of her walk with God and even strongly suggested that her only true interest in the church was the young pastor.

I have also counseled and encouraged men who, after accepting Jesus as their Lord, found themselves being slandered on the job. Fellow workers who once had been buddies began a campaign of innuendos and lies that sometimes cost the men their jobs.

Not only is slander a powerful tool of the devil and of religion; it is also a very dangerous tool in our own hands as well. How often we have ruined a person's reputation by saying, "He's a good brother, but...." We need not complete the sentence. We have already cast doubt on the integrity of that brother (or sister). It is slander by inference.

People will often suffer slander by association. We saw this when two of our best-known television evangelists were exposed for immoral conduct. One of them was also convicted of mishandling donated funds. Whatever measure of guilt may have been involved, the public lost confidence in all preachers who used television as their platform. Television stations cancelled some Christian programs that had run for years. Even local churches reported a tremendous drop in their income and attendance. The sin of a few visible ministers was projected onto all who preached the gospel, and the slander hurt the body of Christ in America far more than the sin of the two very visible preachers.

What can we do when someone deliberately or inferentially slanders us? The more we protest our innocence, the more people think we are guilty. The weapon of slander works quickly; the defense against it works slowly. Often by the time the person being slandered is aware of the attack, the damage has already been done. The more they try to prove their innocence, the more they are judged guilty. In condemnation others say, "Where there's smoke, there's fire," and any attempts at self-justification are seen as a smoke screen to prevent discovering the fire.

We must live so that the slander is seen to be a lie, but, of course, some people will not even look at us again once they believe the slander. Slander doesn't need a shred of truth in it to be effective. It just needs to be projected in a believable manner, and some persons have an uncanny ability to make you believe that whatever they say is true.

The important thing for each of us to learn is how to handle that slander inwardly. It is a very sharp piece of sand that will continue to cut for years until internal (emotional) bleeding causes spiritual death. Like Marvin the oyster, we need to isolate the slander in a protective sac and then pour protective layers of spiritual nacre around that foreign intrusion until we have a smooth, round pearl instead of the painful grain of defamation.

There is no justice in slander, so there is no wisdom in trying to seek out its roots. Comfort comes in knowing that it is a lie and that it can be covered by listening to the truth that God speaks about us. If we are living in His righteousness and in His approval, we can live with the slander and disapproval of others. This may not reverse the pain that the slander initially inflicted, but it will protect us from the further pain of its intrusion.

It may also help us to stop seeking the approval of other people. Success is always a threat to the less successful. Your victory is never sweet to one who lives in

The Irritation of Slander

defeat. Often slander flows out of being jealous or threatened, and these are motives over which we have very little control in the lives of others. We must learn to live in the approval of the Lord and expect a measure of disapproval by others. On His way to Calvary, Jesus said:

> For if they do these things in a green tree,
> what shall be done in the dry? (Luke 23:31).

It should never come as a shock to be slandered for righteousness' sake. Slander is the tool used when nothing else seems to discredit us.

We can also be encouraged by the fact that we are neither the first nor the last to endure slander because of our walk with God. David encountered it. Maybe his handling of it can give us guidelines. He wrote:

> For I have heard the slander of many: fear was on every side: while they took counsel together against me, they devised to take away my life. But I trusted in thee, O Lord: I said, Thou art my God. My times are in thy hand: deliver me from the hand of mine enemies, and from them that persecute me. Make thy face to shine upon thy servant: save me for thy mercies' sake (Psalm 31:13-16).

When we suffer at the hand of slanderers, we can take courage in knowing that they must realize we could not be bought off or caused to join them. If we were not such a threat to them, they wouldn't bother to slander us. We can also take comfort in knowing that the slanderer is in the hand of God — vengeance is His, not ours. Wise Solomon said:

87

> He that hideth hatred with lying lips, and he that uttereth a slander, is a fool (Proverbs 10:18).

When dealing with slander, David prayed:

> Let me not be ashamed, O Lord; for I have called upon thee: let the wicked be ashamed, and let them be silent in the grave. Let the lying lips be put to silence; which speak grievous things proudly and contemptuously against the righteous (Psalm 31:17-18).

Following Jesus has consistently produced salvos of slander, but His indwelling life answers that attack by helping us make a pearl out of the intruding irritant.

Most slander is malicious, but some of it comes out of unbelief. Jesus faced such stubborn unbelief in the persons to whom He ministered that it became a nagging irritant to Him. His response shows us what to do when we, too, encounter unbelief, as we will discover in the next chapter. O

CHAPTER EIGHT

THE IRRITATION OF UNBELIEF

THE MINISTRY AND MESSAGE of Jesus consistently caused people to marvel and be amazed. We read that the disciples marvelled repeatedly at Jesus and His works. Both Jews and Gentiles marvelled at Jesus. The multitudes who embraced Him marvelled, and His accusers who hated Him also marvelled at Him. Even the Pharisees, the governor and Pilate marvelled and wondered at Jesus. This should not be too surprising, for God had declared through His prophet:

> Behold ye among the heathen, and regard, and wonder marvellously: for I will work a work in your days, which ye will not believe, though it be told you (Habakkuk 1:5).

Seeing is not necessarily believing. Even in heaven there will be expressions of marvel at the works of God, for we read:

> And they sing the song of Moses the servant
> of God, and the song of the Lamb, saying,
> Great and marvelous are thy works, Lord
> God Almighty; just and true are thy ways,
> thou King of saints (Revelation 15:3).

The more we come to know Jesus, the greater our
sense of wonder becomes. Eternity itself is too short to
exhaust our sensation of awe when we see the magnificence of our God. This kind of marvelling pleases God.

Still, in another sense of the word, Jesus challenged His
listeners to "marvel not." The first time was to Nicodemus, who had sought out Jesus at night. He told him:

> Marvel not that I said unto thee, Ye must be
> born again (John 3:7).

The second time was to the Jews who angrily sought
to kill Jesus because He said that God was His father.
He told them:

> Marvel not at this: for the hour is coming, in
> the which all that are in the graves shall hear
> his voice (John 5:28).

In both cases Jesus was simply saying that their marvelling evidenced unbelief rather than faith.

Sometimes human nature caused Jesus to marvel.
Luke tells of a centurion who sent a message asking
Jesus to come heal a sick servant. While Jesus was on
the way to fulfill this request, the centurion sent word
that he was unworthy to have Christ as a guest in his
house, but he was assured that if Jesus merely said the
word, the servant would be healed. Having faced such a
high level of unbelief among His own people, Jesus was

pleased to see such a high level of belief in this centurion. Luke records:

> When Jesus heard these things, he marvelled at him, and turned him about, and said unto the people that followed him, I say unto you, I have not found so great faith, no, not in Israel (Luke 7:9).

The second time we read of Jesus marvelling, He did so because of a *lack* of faith in the people. Mark tells us:

> And he marvelled because of their unbelief. And he went round about the villages, teaching (Mark 6:6).

This sense of amazement never left Jesus. With all the amazing miracles He performed and the life-giving teaching He shared, the people still would not believe. Their unbelief consistently astonished Jesus. More than this, it deeply wounded Him. It was an irritant that He could not expel from His life.

The unbelief that caused this pain was varied. Some in the multitudes believed only while they witnessed miracles.

> Then said Jesus unto him, Except ye see signs and wonders, ye will not believe (John 4:48).

These demonstrations of power did not produce lasting faith in the observers. When the miracles ended and the teaching began, their faith vanished. Their hearts were like sieves — faith poured straight through.

We still have people like this among us. They are

intrigued by the miraculous and the supernatural, but they remain unchanged in their faith toward Jesus. This causes pain to the church, and it remains an irritant to Christ Jesus as well.

Other followers of Jesus refused to believe in spite of what they saw. Jesus said of them:

> But I said unto you, That ye also have seen me, and believe not (John 6:36).

His self-revelation had not produced lasting faith in these people. This so irritated Jesus that He even questioned whether His disciples had come into true faith.

> From that time many of his disciples went back, and walked no more with him. Then said Jesus unto the twelve, Will ye also go away? Then Simon Peter answered him, Lord, to whom shall we go? thou hast the words of eternal life. And we believe and are sure that thou art that Christ, the Son of the living God (John 6:66-69).

How comforting and reassuring it must have been to hear such a declaration of faith in the face of abandonment. Sometimes Christian workers barely survive the pain of losing followers to backsliding. Similarly, parents agonize over unbelief in their grown children. They search within themselves for something they did wrong in raising their children. Jesus knew what each of us must learn. You cannot force a person to maintain his or her faith in God. If Jesus lost followers to faithlessness, we shouldn't expect to keep everyone who makes an initial confession of faith. Paul warned his spiritual son Timothy:

> Now the Spirit speaketh expressly, that in the
> latter times some shall depart from the faith,
> giving heed to seducing spirits, and doctrines
> of devils (1 Timothy 4:1).

Our lives are not governed by truth. They are governed by what we believe, for what we believe becomes our belief system. If we choose to believe a lie, that becomes the governing principle by which we live, in spite of what we may see or know about the truth. Any of us could be seduced away from the truth in Christ Jesus.

Sometimes even those people who were closest to Jesus wouldn't believe. We read:

> For neither did his brethren believe in him
> (John 7:5).

> Is not this the carpenter's son? is not his
> mother called Mary? and his brethren, James,
> and Joses, and Simon, and Judas? (Matthew
> 13:55).

It is painful to have to fight unbelief in your own hometown. How His enemies must have thrown it in the face of Jesus that His stepbrothers, who probably knew Him best, didn't believe in Him. The citizens of Nazareth insisted that Jesus couldn't be more than they had experienced while He was growing up among them.

We Christians also face this pain when a member of our immediate household or family refuses to join us in our faith or they won't believe that our faith is real. A prophet is seldom honored in his hometown.

Even His disciples, who had participated in His miracles, had seasons of lapsing into unbelief instead of living in faith. We read:

> Afterward he appeared unto the eleven as
> they sat at meat, and upbraided them with
> their unbelief and hardness of heart, because
> they believed not them which had seen him
> after he was risen (Mark 16:14).

It pained Jesus deeply that His own disciples, who
had been with Him for three years, couldn't maintain
faith. Christian leaders today are still shocked to discover deep-seated unbelief in their associates and
friends. It usually does not surface until negative circumstances or external pressures challenge their faith.
Sometimes they discover that they had lived under the
umbrella of another's faith; but when they had to exercise that faith, they found themselves to be full of unbelief.

Often our initial response is, If that person can't believe, what hope is there for the rest of the congregation? The apostle John was accurate in saying:

> He came unto his own, and his own received
> him not (John 1:11).

But why were so many people unbelieving in spite of
what seems to be conclusive evidence to us? Jesus gave
three reasons:

He worded the *first* reason in the form of a question:

> How can ye believe, which receive honor one
> of another, and seek not the honor that
> cometh from God only? (John 5:44).

Whenever people are more concerned about being

accepted by others than about receiving God's approval, they block off the flow of faith God seeks to give to them. In the days of Jesus, many refused to believe, for it would cause their expulsion from the existing religious system. They wanted the honor and praise of their associates more than they wanted the life of God. Things haven't changed much.

Jesus gave a *second* and far more devastating reason for deliberate unbelief:

> But ye believe not, because ye are not of my sheep, as I said unto you (John 10:26).

Not everyone who witnesses miracles has been transformed by the saving grace of Jesus. Our churches are filled with people who are convinced but not converted. Those who are not Christ's sheep will not believe. Perhaps they cannot believe, for what they see and hear involves a life about which they know nothing. People will not come into the kingdom of God through the route of education. God's route is through transformation. Jesus told Nicodemus:

> Except a man be born again, he cannot see the kingdom of God...Marvel not that I said unto thee, Ye must be born again (John 3:3,7).

Until we have His nature, we cannot flow in His faith.

The *third* reason Jesus gave for the unbelief of the people was:

> And ye have not his word abiding in you: for whom he hath sent, him ye believe not (John 5:38).

Faith's foundation is the Word of God, not observation of the supernatural. Paul declared:

> So then faith cometh by hearing, and hearing
> by the word of God (Romans 10:17).

Those who honored Christ's miracles but did not heed His Word had little more than emotion upon which to base their faith, and emotion consistently runs hot and cold.

Jesus knew these three reasons for the lack of faith, but it grieved Him deeply. He also knew the ultimate results of unbelief.

1. Unbelief greatly limited Christ's ministry among them.

> And he did not many mighty works there because of their unbelief (Matthew 13:58).

2. Unbelief prevents people from learning spiritual principles.

> If I have told you earthly things, and ye believe not, how shall ye believe, if I tell you of heavenly things? (John 3:12).

3. Unbelief results in eternal death instead of life.

> I said therefore unto you, that ye shall die in your sins: for if ye believe not that I am he, ye shall die in your sins (John 8:24).

The unbelief of many people caused Jesus pain, but He never lost faith in Himself because of it. He knew who He was and what His mission on earth was. The

Father's approval more than compensated for the disapproval of these faithless people. Rather than reject them, He continued to love them, to minister to them and to offer them teaching. The great love of God within Him acted as spiritual nacre to cover this irritant of unbelief until it formed another magnificent pearl.

Each of us will face unbelief. It always hurts — sometimes more than others. But we cannot isolate ourselves from the world. We are the salt. We are the witnesses. Whether they believe or not, God will be just in the day of judgment. This is God's plan, but it does not insulate us against the pain of their unbelief. It should help us to remember that many people did not believe Jesus either.

The deepest hurts come from those who are closest to us, especially an unbelieving husband or wife. Sometimes the pain is so great that divorce seems a sensible solution. Still, Paul taught:

> But to the rest speak I, not the Lord: If any brother hath a wife that believeth not, and she be pleased to dwell with him, let him not put her away. And the woman which hath an husband that believeth not, and if he be pleased to dwell with her, let her not leave him (1 Corinthians 7:12-13).

The Bible does not teach that conversion is grounds for divorce. Quite the opposite, for it says:

> For the unbelieving husband is sanctified by the wife, and the unbelieving wife is sanctified by the husband: else were your children unclean; but now are they holy (1 Corinthians 7:14).

Rather than let their unbelief dilute our faith, we actually become an agent for sanctifying the unbeliever. God's blessing upon our lives flows over to the unbelieving mate. There may be pain to bear, but there are blessings to share.

Doris Barber (not her real name) came to our church when our membership was about three years old. She had a pleasant smile that masked a deep hurt. I noticed how easily she went into tears during a service, and after she became more comfortable among us she consistently asked for prayer for her unsaved husband.

She seldom missed a prayer service and proved to be an earnest intercessor in prayer, but she always seemed burdened. Sometimes when I looked at her, I visualized a donkey with a heavy load tied onto its back that was never unloaded. She declared that her burden was for her unsaved husband.

As I got to know her better, I learned that her husband was a professional man who was held in high esteem in our area. She used to work in his office before she got saved, but after she met Jesus she could not stand her husband's way of life. So she quit work to get away from him. Unfortunately that wasn't sufficient. She withdrew socially and sexually from her husband. For thirty-five years she isolated herself from him while pleading with him to "get saved."

When she came to me for counsel, I pointed out to her that salvation had changed her, not her husband. He was still the man she had married. While she was pleading with God to change him into what she now wanted, she was completely rejecting him.

"Why would any man want to accept a Jesus who had taken his wife away?" I asked her. "You've made Jesus a competitor."

"I didn't mean to do that," she replied, "I just want

him to get saved. His unbelief has wounded me more deeply than you will ever know. I hurt all the time."

"So you have rejected him to ease the pain?" I asked.

"I guess so," she said.

Slowly I helped her to see that she would never win her husband by displaying her pain, but she might reach him by sharing the love of Christ with him. "Have you ever tried loving him with God's love?" I asked her.

"But he doesn't believe in God," she said. "His unbelief has tied my hands."

"Did Thomas's unbelief immobilize Jesus?" I asked. "Did He isolate Himself from him and mourn over his unbelief, or did He lovingly come to Thomas and accommodate his unbelief until all his doubts were removed?"

She saw my point. To her husband's shock and pleasure, she began to love him again after thirty-five years. Their home is again secure, and she is no longer the martyr asking us to pray for her husband's salvation. She covered her deep hurt with God's love and made a pearl out of it.

Has her husband accepted Jesus? Not yet, but the home is in order, the pain is gone, and the pearl of love is consistently displayed. The story has not yet ended, but this book must go to press. Perhaps when we get to heaven, we will see Doris and her husband standing hand in hand before the throne of God as she presents to Jesus the pearl this pain eventually produced. If, however, he should choose to remain an unbeliever to the end, Doris will have rid herself of the pain and will still have a beautiful jewel to present to her Savior.

God has not promised to change all our circumstances to please us. He would have to violate the free will of others to do so. Yet He has promised to change us and our relationship to these circumstances. His Word says:

> But we all, with open face beholding as in a
> glass the glory of the Lord, are changed into
> the same image from glory to glory, even as
> by the Spirit of the Lord (2 Corinthians 3:18).

Much as a grain of sand is transformed "from glory to glory" by the oyster's secretion of nacre, so God's Spirit within us effects radical changes that bring forth radiant beauty to replace irritating unbelief.

Most of our churches have one or more Doris Barber — women who live in the pain of great unbelief in the home. Often the husband or the children don't believe. The women yearn to see their loved ones enjoy Christ Jesus as they have come to enjoy Him, but the pain of unbelief causes them to bleed nearly to death spiritually. The irritant produces an infection instead of a pearl. They won't let the love of Christ come into their hearts to allow His nacre of divine love to cover the irritant until it stops hurting.

There is rarely anything attractive about being a "Doris." She wears her pain on her face and expresses it in her every conversation. Her anxiety for good becomes a negative phobia that focuses on the bad or unpleasant and produces disabling stress. Not only is she miserable, but she shares her misery with anyone who will listen to her. No one doubts her pain, but everyone around her wishes she would learn to form a pearl around this pain of unbelief instead of constantly playing the role of a martyr "for Christ's sake." After all, God did promise:

> To appoint unto them that mourn in Zion, to
> give unto them beauty for ashes, the oil of
> joy for mourning, the garment of praise for
> the spirit of heaviness; that they might be

called trees of righteousness, the planting of
the Lord, that he might be glorified (Isaiah
61:3).

Serving God does not guarantee exemption from the
fires that reduce our plans to ashes, or sorrows and dis-
appointments that bring mourning and overwhelming
heaviness to our spirits. Pain is part of living. When we
make an abrupt change in our way of life after accepting
Jesus as our personal Savior, some who were very close
to us before our conversion may reject us completely.
They do not understand us, and they do not want to have
anything to do with whatever or Whomever has made
such radical changes in our behavior. Their rejection of
both us and the gospel can be an irritant that burns like
a fire and depresses us like the death of a loved one.
However, if we refuse to become irritated, we can find
beauty, joy and praise available in exchange for our
ashes, mourning and the spirit of heaviness.

Even Jesus did not bring everyone to faith in spite of
who He was and what He did. Neither will we. Instead
of dwelling on this failure, Jesus refused to allow the
unbelief of others to destroy His participation in life. He
set the example for us by handling this painful irritant
with such love as to form pearls of beauty that bless
those who notice them.

Not all who fall into unbelief become atheists. Many
of them merely substitute something for their lack of
faith. Religious substitution became a constant irritant
to Jesus. O

CHAPTER NINE

THE IRRITATION OF RELIGIOUS SUBSTITUTION

PARTIALLY BECAUSE OF a heavy travel schedule that allows him only a few days home each month and partially as the result of his boyhood habits, Judson is a mail-order zealot. He is on more mailing lists than you can imagine. But he says that when the order blank contains the statement: "We reserve the right to make substitutions if the item you ordered is out of stock," he throws the catalogue away. This statement legalizes the old "bait-and-switch" ploy where a quality item is advertised, but a much lower quality product is actually delivered.

Far too many Christians reserve the right to make substitutions in their relationships and dealings with God. When they have little or no faith, they bring feelings or formulas to Him. If they seem unable to come to God with repentance, they approach Him with remorse. The ingenuity some Christians display in producing a substitute may be admirable, but the surrogate product is never admissible in God's presence.

The greatest tragedy of religious substitution is its needlessness. Where one portion of the Bible commands us to bring something specific to God, another portion offers that same thing to us as a gift. For instance, we read in the book of Acts:

> And the times of this ignorance God winked at; but now commandeth all men every where to repent (Acts 17:30).

To balance this, Paul urged Timothy:

> In meekness instructing those that oppose themselves; if God peradventure will give them repentance to the acknowledging of the truth (2 Timothy 2:25).

First God commands repentance, then He offers it as a gift. This is a case where if you cannot come to God *with* what He requires, come to God *for* what He requires. God will give repentance to those who will acknowledge the truth so that they need not substitute remorse or regret when they come into God's presence.

This same principle works with faith. The writer to the Hebrews declares:

> But without faith it is impossible to please him: for he that cometh to God must believe that He is, and that He is a rewarder of them that diligently seek Him (Hebrews 11:6).

For those times when we seem to be totally without faith, we can take courage, for:

> Faith...is the gift of God (Ephesians 2:8).

> To one is given by the Spirit...faith (1 Corin-
> thians 12:8-9).

When we cannot come to the Lord *with* faith, we can come to Him *for* faith. There is no need for substitution.

This needless substitution of something of human quality for that which God has provided was illustrated in the story Jesus told of a royal wedding (see Matthew 22:1-14). Consistent with the custom of the day and the financial ability of this king, special wedding garments were provided for all the guests. When the king came in to enjoy the marriage celebration of his son, he spotted a guest who was not wearing a provided wedding garment. The man had substituted his own garment.

This guest looked as out of place as a bridesmaid would look in a modern wedding if she wore a black evening dress while the rest of the bridesmaids wore pink taffeta knee-length dresses. The penalty for substituting a wedding garment at this king's wedding celebration was severe.

> Then said the king to the servants, Bind him
> hand and foot, and take him away, and cast
> him into outer darkness; there shall be weep-
> ing and gnashing of teeth (Matthew 22:13).

In this case, at least, substitution was deadly. Was Jesus referring to His Father as the King and Himself as the Son who was being married to His bride, the church? If so, it could be tragic to enter God's presence with substitutes for His provisions.

During the ministry of Jesus, He was constantly irritated by these substitutions. He often directed His remarks to the religious leaders, but what He said also applied to the people who blindly followed them in their substitutionary actions.

One substitution that irritated Jesus to the point of anger was making God's house of prayer become a den of thieves. He said:

> It is written, My house shall be called the house of prayer; but ye have made it a den of thieves (Matthew 21:13; see Mark 11:17, Luke 19:46).

Jesus was angered that commercialism had replaced communion with God. The combination of divine zeal and the inner awareness that His time to die had arrived caused Jesus to act very much out of character. We read:

> And when he had made a scourge of small cords, he drove them all out of the temple, and the sheep, and the oxen; and poured out the changers' money, and overthrew the tables (John 2:15).

It was one man against the temple merchandisers. What fury must have been in His eyes! What authority His voice must have possessed! Long before His whip stung their backs, His words had pierced their consciences to such a degree that they had no strength with which to resist Him.

Christ directed His anger against the hub of a degenerate religious system that had put ease of performance ahead of God's expressed purpose for the temple — fellowship with the God of love.

Matthew, Mark and John say that Jesus overthrew the tables of the money changers, but John adds that Jesus deliberately poured out the money from the money bags. We can imagine the mad scramble by these merchants to retrieve their money. They were probably elbowing away the Jews who had been waiting to trade Roman coins for the temple coin. As they struggled to retrieve the rolling coins, they felt the stinging lash of Jesus' handmade whip. Before long, pain outweighed greed, and they all scurried for the exit.

He not only drove out those who *sold*, but Matthew says He also drove out those who *bought* (see Matthew 21:12). He knew that the entire commercial traffic in the temple was a matter of convenience. People didn't want to be bothered bringing a gift to the Lord; it was easier to pick it up in the outer court of the temple after they arrived. This was not a service of the heart. It was mechanical service done out of religious duty, and the easier and faster they could do it, the better.

The scene reminds me of the modern "worshipper" who attends the Sunday morning service, tips God in the offering plate and complains if the service goes beyond noon. There is no heart for God and no faith in His provisions. These worshippers are not responding to a love for God. They attend public worship as insurance against hell. They offer a perfunctory gift as a substitute for praise, prayer and worship. All such substitutions are unacceptable to God.

Another substitute that annoyed Jesus was public displays in place of personal devotion. He contrasted the prayers of the Pharisee and the publican:

> The Pharisee stood and prayed thus with himself, God, I thank thee, that I am not as other men are, extortioners, unjust, adulterers, or even as this publican. And the publican, standing afar off, would not lift up so much as his eyes unto heaven, but smote upon his breast, saying, God be merciful to

me a sinner (Luke 18:11,13).

This public display and declaration of righteousness by the religious leaders was a constant irritant to Jesus. He exposed the true nature of the scribes and Pharisees:

> Ye devour widows' houses, and for a pretence make long prayer: therefore ye shall receive the greater damnation (Matthew 23:14).

As a pastor I have seen some people go to great lengths to show public piety to salve their consciences for their unrighteous living. God doesn't respond to a beautiful prayer if the praying man has abused his wife or children the night before or if the praying woman has cheated on her husband during the week.

I have also observed that some people will make quite a public display of their giving as a subterfuge for the inconsistencies of their lives. Jesus spoke of devoted religious persons who:

> ...pay tithe of mint and anise and cummin, and have omitted the weightier matters of the law, judgment, mercy, and faith: these ought ye to have done, and not to leave the other undone (Matthew 23:23).

They gave impeccable performances, even to the point of tithing the salt and pepper on the table, but in their devotion to God they were impaired. They became masters at display, but lacked devotion.

Still a third way religious substitution provoked Jesus was the Jews' propensity to substitute lecture for living. They were open to listen to the teachers of the law. Multitudes flocked to hear the preaching of John the Baptist, and even larger crowds followed Jesus from place to place. At times the people seemed mesmerized by the teaching of Jesus. At least once (and probably more often), they stayed so long that:

> Jesus called his disciples unto him, and said, I have compassion on the multitude, because they continue with me now three days, and have nothing to eat: and I will not send them away fasting, lest they faint in the way (Matthew 15:32).

For three hundred or more years the Jews had been without an anointed prophet, priest or king. When Jesus came with this anointing, He engendered excitement. Even His enemies had to testify, "Never man spake like this man" (John 7:46).

His words flowed like a refreshing stream in a wilderness area, and the people were happy to drink in those words as long as He would talk. But when those words called for action, we read:

> Many therefore of his disciples, when they had heard this, said, This is an hard saying; who can hear it? ...From that time many of his disciples went back, and walked no more with him (John 6:60,66).

They didn't mind listening to Him, but they had substituted listening for actively living what they were hearing.

Jesus told His disciples, "If ye know these things, happy are ye if ye do them" (John 13:17). He knew that it was not the hearing of the ear but the determination of the heart that would effect change in human behavior. God is not pleased by what we learn, but by what we *do* with what we learn.

Parents and teachers everywhere will attest to the fact that children tend to listen attentively as a substitute for letting what is heard actually change their behavior. Is there a parent alive who has never said, "How many times do I have to tell you?" We, too, need to cover this irritation with a protective layer of spiritual nacre to prevent it from becoming inwardly destructive, just as Peter tells us:

> And above all things have fervent charity among yourselves: for charity shall cover the multitude of sins (1 Peter 4:8).

Just as Jesus continued to love these avid listeners in spite of their unwillingness to do anything about what they were hearing, so we must continue to love others enough to tell them the same thing over and over. We dare not cease to teach and train others, no matter how slowly they seem to change, for James reminds us:

> Let him know, that he which converteth the sinner from the error of his way shall save a soul from death, and shall hide a multitude of sins (James 5:20).

Still a fourth way in which the people practiced religious substitution was in replacing internal purity with external holiness. Jesus lashed out against this repeatedly. He said:

> Woe unto you, scribes and Pharisees, hypocrites! for ye make clean the outside of the

cup and of the platter, but within they are full of extortion and excess. Thou blind Pharisee, cleanse first that which is within the cup and platter, that the outside of them may be clean also (Matthew 23:25-26).

Changing His metaphor, Jesus strengthened His denunciation of hypocrisy by saying:

Woe unto you, scribes and Pharisees, hypocrites! for ye are like unto whited sepulchres, which indeed appear beautiful outward, but are within full of dead men's bones, and of all uncleanness. Even so ye also outwardly appear righteous unto men, but within ye are full of hypocrisy and iniquity (Matthew 23:27-28).

You need not be a student of the Greek language to get the full impact of Christ's message. Jesus was aggravated with hypocrisy. There is no place for pretense in dealing with God. While in prayer, we are either talking to God or we are not. If we are, it is prayer. If we are not, we should not hypocritically put it in a prayer format. Similarly, we need not make a display of our devotion. Others don't need to see what we are doing for God. Three times in one discourse Jesus said that the Father will openly reward secret acts of piety:

1) That thine alms may be in secret: and thy Father which seeth in secret himself shall reward thee openly.
2) But thou, when thou prayest, enter into thy closet, and when thou hast shut thy door, pray to thy Father which is in secret; and thy

Father which seeth in secret shall reward thee
openly.

　3) That thou appear not unto men to fast,
but unto thy Father which is in secret: and thy
Father, which seeth in secret, shall reward
thee openly (Matthew 6:4,6,18).

Religious people in Christ's day, as well as in our
time, tend to want the praise without paying the price.
They tout their false Christianity as if it were genuine in
the same way counterfeit manufacturers put others' la-
bels on their cheap merchandise.

This inferior religious contraband may have deceived
the people, but Jesus wasn't fooled. In order to have the
pure and holy, He simply made the hillsides, gardens
and seashores places of prayer and ministry. He covered
the irritating fake with the genuine. He withdrew from
false religiosity to participate in loving communication
with His Father. His all-night seasons of fellowship
with God occurred wherever He could find privacy. He
didn't need the trappings of the religious system.

The consistent substitution of outer holiness for internal purity deeply pained Jesus. But He turned His
pain into a pearl by confining this irritation in a protective sac, as the oyster does, and not allowing it to damage other areas of His life. Then He released the
spiritual nacre of a real relationship with God and
formed a pearl that could be thought of as the first gate
in the western wall of the New Jerusalem.

Although greatly angered at the religious substitution
that bred hypocrisy, Jesus was able to direct His anger
toward the violators without allowing it to disturb His
relationship with His Father. We must learn to do so,
too. Religious hypocrites have a way of sticking out like
a bandage on a preacher's pointing finger on Sunday

morning. We can easily turn our eyes toward them instead of keeping them on God. If there is anything we can learn from hypocrites it is to be honest in our spiritual relationships.

The American press tends to publicize our most notorious religious hypocrites. When we read and see how they have pretended for the sake of money, position and power, we can become disgusted with the whole religious realm. We need to realize that no one makes counterfeit pennies. They only counterfeit something worthwhile. The presence of hypocrites only emphasizes that there must be something valuable in a pure relationship with God through Jesus Christ.

Rather than rebel at religion because we see the irritating substitution of the false for the real, we can learn from these bad examples and set our hearts to know God in purity and righteousness. It actually takes more work to pretend than to be real. And being real requires far less memory work. No person has a good enough memory to consistently live a lie.

Instead of wounding our lives with rebellion because of the pretense of some, we should hear the plea of Paul's heart when he wrote:

> I beseech you therefore, brethren, by the mercies of God, that ye present your bodies a living sacrifice, holy, acceptable unto God, which is your reasonable service (Romans 12:1).

This will not only help us make a pearl out of the irritation of religious substitution, but it will help us face the intrusive irritation of submission to the will of God. The next chapter shows how Jesus Himself had to struggle with submission while He lived on earth. O

CHAPTER TEN

THE IRRITATION OF SUBMISSION

THE URGE TO MAKE substitutions in our lives probably comes from a strong desire to "do things my way." But the heart of Christian commitment is submission to the will of God in all things. Almost invariably we speak of the will of man *versus* the will of God, but the New Testament speaks far more of the two wills blending into one action than of the two battling for territory.

Did you know that Jesus faced frustration at having to submit consciously to the will of the Father? Let's look at His pre-incarnate existence. There Jesus functioned in a monopoly where there was but one will in existence — God's will. God's wish was automatically heaven's command, and none ever questioned the divine will. Out of this will flowed a harmony unknown to mankind. God's will was as natural as sunrise and sunset and even more beneficial to His creation and His creatures. The outstanding characteristic of eternity is this one will.

Rebellion rose up in the midst of this unity. Lucifer exercised his will against the known will of the Father. This violated the authority of God's monopolistic will, disgracing, dishonoring and defiling the peace, harmony and unity of eternity. Where there had always been but one will, there were now two wills. God's response to this was extensive, for not only was Satan cast out of heaven, but eternity was interrupted with a parenthesis that we call *time*.

The fundamental difference between time and eternity is the number of wills that are extant. Time began with the introduction of a second will (Satan's) to the will of God, and when Adam exercised his will by choosing to sin, it caused a third will to come into existence. Later, Cain's jealousy and the murder of his brother Abel introduced a fourth will and so on.

There were millions of wills operating hourly by the time Jesus entered His ministry. No wonder His (and our) generation lived in such confusion and disorder, for just as a home verges on the brink of chaos when the growing children reject the will of the parents and impose their wills upon the household, so God's creation groans under the weight of opposing wills.

Jesus knew that time is but a parenthesis — a temporary experience. God's Spirit is at work in the lives of believers to bring our wills into conformity with the will of God. At the end of time, God resolves to so subdue the godless and the satanic forces that they will submit to the divine will in everything. When all wills have surrendered to God's one will, "there should be time no longer" (Revelation 10:6). There will come an end to the delays God has endured while allowing multiple wills to operate. When all kingdoms have become "the kingdoms of our Lord, and of his Christ; and he shall reign forever and ever" (Revelation 11:15), then time will give way to eternity.

While the Holy Spirit within Jesus shared this knowledge with Him, the practical reality was that the will of the Father was consistently being violated by His special creation — mankind. Jesus could see that God's slightest expression was still the law of the universe for all His angels. He experienced how creation is in complete and immediate obedience to God's will. Water turned into wine, congealed for Jesus to walk on, and became calm in the midst of a storm — all in response to a spoken word. The Lord knew that creation now groans under the curse that man's exercise of self-will has imposed upon it (see Romans 8:20-23), but it has never rebelled against God's will.

During His ministry Jesus discovered that even the demonic realm, as opposed to God as it is, obeyed His voice every time He expressed the will of God concerning it. Satan can function only within the boundaries God has set for him, and he never may step beyond them.

No, it was not the angelic, the satanic or the created universe that Jesus found in rebellion against the known will of God. It was mankind whose consistent prayer seemed to be: "Nevertheless, not Thy will, but mine, be done." Jesus had more difficulty asking people to surrender their wills to God than the government has recruiting volunteers for the armed forces in times of peace.

Jesus was irritated to see such resistance in surrendering to God's will. Jesus understood far better than we do that the issue is never which will is greater, but which will is desirable. Any thinking person would admit that God's will is vastly superior, for among many other things it is based on total knowledge. God's omniscience is the perfect basis for the exercise of a will.

Nothing is beyond the scope of His knowledge, and the past and the future are as vivid and real to Him as the present is to us.

Also, God's will is based on a master plan for the church — Christ's body here on the earth. God's will is never capricious, nor is it emotional. It is based on a predetermined plan that benefits God and man, heaven and earth, time and eternity. Believers are not asked to submit to this master will blindly, for Paul assured us that God has:

> ...made known unto us the mystery of his will, according to his good pleasure which he hath purposed in himself: That in the dispensation of the fulness of times he might gather together in one all things in Christ, both which are in heaven, and which are on earth; even in him (Ephesians 1:9-10).

God is going to bring everything together again in Christ Jesus — all wills, all purposes, all plans and all covenant people.

This, of course, had not happened by the time Christ came, nor has it yet happened on earth. Obviously God's will is not the only will operating in the world today. God has granted man the right to a free will, and nothing in His redemptive plan has negated this provision. One great contrast between the work of the demonic and the work of the divine is that the demonic wants to make man's will inoperative, while God insists that the will of man remain operative. Satan functions better in a man if he can induce a trance-like state of mindlessness, but every operation of God in and through mankind requires the operation of man's will. God did not create robots; He created man in the divine image, which includes an operative will. He desires for the will of man to be harmonious with the divine will, not to be vacated. Even the ecstatic gift of tongues needs the operation of man's will, not a mindless emptying of the will to the spirit world, for as we read concerning the initial experience:

> And they were all filled with the Holy Ghost, and began to speak with other tongues, as the Spirit gave them utterance (Acts 2:4).

They spoke; the Spirit gave them the words. This is divine and human action harmoniously flowing in one will. Jesus learned this through trial and error. He lived in such union with the Father's will that He could testify:

> And he that sent me is with me: the Father hath not left me alone; for I do always those things that please him (John 8:29).

Learning to submit to the Father's will as a human man was difficult for Jesus in that it was not a one-time commitment. Jesus learned that submission is not deactivation. The whole of the Scriptures calls for the continual activation of man's will. "Whosoever will...." (Revelation 22:17) involves both permission from the divine side and activation on man's part.

Jesus knew that most of God's promises are conditional. When man activates his will to meet those conditions, God activates His will to supply the promised grace. God's favorite way of answering prayer is "I will, if you will." God has not provided for passivity in the life of the Christian; He has called for activity. When we arise, God arises. When we live according to His will, the forces of heaven become available to us, but as long as we are merely wishing instead of willing, nothing happens beyond emotional stirring. In this realm the renewed emphasis upon faith has blessed the body of Christ. Believers are being encouraged to "put legs to their prayers" and "action to their asking." It is not that we can coerce God into action, but we can actively co-operate with Him.

Even in times of discipline the individual's will must be activated. Every time Pharaoh repented under the pressure of the plagues, Moses would ask him when he wanted the plague removed. In the case of the miserable plague of frogs, Pharaoh said, "Tomorrow" (see Exodus 8:10). He was content to spend one more night with the frogs before surrendering his will to the will of God. All too frequently, so are we. God waits for our wills to surrender to His will before lifting the pressure He has exerted to direct us into that will.

Similarly, when Satan opposes a Christian, that believer must exercise his or her will against the enemy before God counters the attack. As long as we grant the demonic powers our permission for them to harass us, God will not intervene. But when we exercise our wills to file a complaint against the enemy, God sends forth His Spirit to liberate us.

With the limitation of our carnal minds, we tend to think that a complete surrender to the will of God guarantees that we will walk in perfect harmony and union with other Christians. This is true if those Christians are also walking in the absolute will of God, but often they are not.

Every Christian is prone to selfishness. This exercise of the self-will in the lives of those Jesus had drawn closest to Him became a major irritant to Him. The disciples squabbled over who would be the greatest in the kingdom. They pled and begged for positions of authority and power in the coming kingdom. Peter actually told Jesus that what He was saying about His approaching death would never happen. Jesus learned that when you share a little authority with people, they often rise to exert far more control than was given.

The will of man is the greatest hindrance to the exercise of the will of God in the church on earth. As the prophet declared:

> All we like sheep have gone astray; *we have turned every one to his own way*; and the Lord hath laid on him the iniquity of us all (Isaiah 53:6, italics added).

Yet God's power is able to rule and overrule the negative effects of our will. He allows our wills to continue to function after we become members of His kingdom. This is also a manifestation of His great grace, for coerced obedience or mindless functioning would be completely unfulfilling to a Christian and would bring no pleasure to God. The plan of redemption was to restore life, not to restrict it, so rather than remove man's will, God released it from the inhibiting power of sin and made it possible for that will to operate in harmony with His will.

This also demonstrated Christ's ability to bear and positively handle pain, for every exercise of the human will against the divine will presents a barrier that God must override. The unsurrendered will of people is basically self-centered and selfish. It often makes a god out of the ego and exerts its authority to bring all desirable things inward. Humanism, which positions man as the total of all things, is little more than the will of man operating without restraints.

If each person's will was merely selfish, that would be disastrous enough to society. But those wills are of necessity based on very limited hindsight, insight and foresight. Most of us learn very little from history or from observing others. We generally base our wills upon the sensory experiences we have had in our lives, so it should be expected that our wills are limited, inaccurate and faulty.

Our capacity for formulating a quality will is as far beneath God's capacity as a two-year-old child's wishes are inferior to the parents' desires. How much better it is for the child to submit to the will of the parents, and how much more beneficial it is for us to submit to the will of God.

Jesus understood that the coming work of the cross was an act of restoration — all that people had forfeited through sin could be restored to them. That is why the Bible calls it a redemptive work. Jesus came to purchase back everything mankind had lost and to restore it freely to us. This includes the free will of men and women; it is this freedom of choice that lifts them above the animal instincts of nature and grants them a little measure of sovereignty, at least over their own lives.

God is absolutely sovereign, and in His sovereignty He purposed to share that supremacy with His children by giving them areas of authority. This does not diminish His dominion; He shares it with us.

Fundamentally, Jesus understood this. The indwelling Holy Spirit was a great teacher. But life, too, is a great instructor. We usually remember more of what we have experienced than what we have heard. Jesus was repeatedly hurt by the exercise of self-will against Him. The religious rulers plotted against Him continually. Followers forsook Him, and His disciples jockeyed for better positions of authority in the coming kingdom. In one breath they would say, "Lord, Lord...," but in the next breath they made themselves lord of their own lives. This had to be irritating to Jesus.

It would be absurd to suggest that Jesus found it personally irritating to submit to the will of God. The irritation to Him was having to submit *consciously*. He was in a human body that resisted the will of God. He was surrounded by human and satanic forces that were openly aligned against God's will, and this pressed on Him. The irritation came because Jesus had to make a deliberate choice to stand with the will of God.

Jesus became a pearlmaker by deliberately and lovingly submitting to the known will of the Father. He did only what He saw His Father do. He declared that He exercised only the judgment that the Father gave to Him. In the garden of Gethsemane He exercised submission in prayer three times: "Not my will, but Thine be done" (Matthew 26:42; Mark 14:36; Luke 22:42). He covered the irritant with complete obedience. The author of the book of Hebrews says:

> Though he were a Son, yet learned he obedience by the things which he suffered (Hebrews 5:8).

The obedience did not produce suffering, for obedience to the will of God is the most peaceful state any of us can enter. During the years that I ran for my life and from the known will of God, I didn't know ten minutes of peace. I knew influence and affluence and enjoyed a financial security better than I had expected, but I did not know peace. Now that I am in the calling of God for my life, my heart knows rest and peace. There is no peace apart from a proper relationship with the Prince of Peace.

Jesus was never separated from this peace. But having to learn deliberate obedience caused Jesus much pain. He had known only the will of the Father until Bethlehem. After that, He had to seek that will and then surrender to it, for He was born with the human capacity to resist God's will. Furthermore, society in His day, both religious and secular, was opposed to the will of God (as is our society). Jesus felt this anti-God pressure as surely as a diver feels the pressure of water as he descends.

In covering this irritation with the nacre of sweet surrender, Jesus produced another beautiful pearl that the Father could have used as a gate for the west wall of the New Jerusalem.

Because of some business dealings that would eventually send me to prison, my wife, daughter and I had to flee to Europe where we hid for one year. We fought the loneliness of separation as a family, but as an emotional safety valve we dedicated each Friday evening to sitting around the fireplace and dreaming of home. We talked of what it would be like to return to America, but never in all those talks did we dare to suggest the possibility of entering the ministry. I was convinced I had ruined every chance of fulfilling the call of God on my life.

When we did return, we rented an apartment in San Jose, California, where I had a few business connections. Although I did not know what I would do, I was so grateful to God for letting me return that I promised Him I would do anything except work for a relative.

After we had purchased some furniture and secured a car, we drove to Salem, Oregon, where my father lay dying. We had been there less than two days when the Lord spoke to my heart that we should move to Salem to assist my brother in his church. He needed my business expertise. I immediately put my wife and daughter in the car and returned to San Jose.

On our way home, my wife wanted to know what had cut my visit so short, especially because it had been nearly three years since I had seen my father. I told her what I felt the Lord had said to me, and I made it very clear that I didn't want to do it. We finished the trip in silence.

My brother called me the next day and said the Lord had impressed on him to invite me to join his staff as the church's business manager. He admitted that he did not have the authority to make this offer, but if I would respond positively, he would call a board meeting and seek this authorization. Assured that this would take a week or more, I told him to call the meeting.

After I hung up the phone, I realized that God was putting me to the test. Would I hold to my terms of "anything but work for a relative," or would I surrender to the will of God?

The next day I was able to get out from under our lease on the apartment. I rented a truck and headed for Salem. By the end of the second day my family and I were settling in a home in Salem. I was so certain of God's will in this matter that I didn't wait for the vote.

When I called my brother the next week to find out the results of the vote, I shocked him by walking into his house fifteen minutes later. I didn't need outer confirmation of God's will. I was positive in my spirit of what God wanted of me, and I found great peace in surrendering to that will. Furthermore, I found myself entering the ministry that I had feared would be withheld from me forever. In my surrender I found myself to be an active participant in the will of God.

As a pastor, I have had to deal with Christians who equated surrendering their wills with being spineless. This serious imbalance will lead to great instability.

God does not want our wills to die. He wants them to come under godly direction. On the one hand we have the sovereign will of God that dares to say, "Before they call, I will answer" (Isaiah 65:24). On the other hand we have the command:

> Call to Me, and I will answer you, and show
> you great and mighty things, which you do
> not know (Jeremiah 33:3, NKJV).

How can we balance the simple will of man with the sublime will of God? Each is a will, but each is not equal. It seems that our wills cannot function without deactivating God's will — and *that* is incomprehensible.

If one child on a seesaw is considerably heavier than the other child, teetering is impossible. The lightweight one must persuade another child to join him on his end of the teeter-totter so that their combined weights equal the weight of the heavier playmate. It takes two to equal one.

This is what God has done through the operation of His Spirit in the life of the believer. We are assured:

> For it is God which worketh in you both to
> will and to do of his good pleasure (Philip-
> pians 2:13).

God's Spirit joins us on our balance board, creating desires in us to do what God wants done. Although the Spirit has motivated our wills, He has not manipulated them. How comfortable it is to be so indwelt by God's Spirit that His will and our wills merge as one. We can be at liberty to do what we want when we have allowed Him to mold that will even before it is expressed.

Rather than veto an expressed will, God prefers to give

spiritual input into that will even before it is fully formulated. This means that short of rebellion or spiritual neglect on man's part, the will of the believer will often parallel the will of God because the active measure of God within us has contributed immeasurably to the formation of that will. Then, like the psalmist, we too can say, "I delight to do thy will, O my God" (Psalm 40:8).

Is it irritating to the flesh of a Christian to submit to the will of God? Of course it is. Yet in handling the irritation of submission with the inner work of the Holy Spirit, we, like Marvin the oyster, can form a pearl that protects.

In oysters, the foreign substance sometimes lodges in muscular tissue. Although a sac or cyst of tissue is formed around it, the muscle action in opening and closing the shell of the oyster continually deforms the shape of the sac, much as squeezing a balloon changes its shape. Although nacre is poured into this sac to form a protective coating around the irritant, it must, of necessity, take on the shape of the sac. Some very irregular shapes result and produce what are called baroque pearls. The difference in their shape makes these pearls unique, but of much less value, for they will not fit well on a string of pearls. A will that submits only under pressure is a lot like a baroque pearl — it is still a pearl, but it is not a perfectly formed one.

We Christians should realize that eventually we will submit to the will of God. The sooner we surrender the more likely we are to form useful pearls.

Refusal to submit to God's perfect will is actually a subtle form of betrayal. Judas did this and sold His Savior for a handful of coins. Jesus' response to this ultimate act of betrayal shows us what we should do when this same irritant invades our lives. O

CHAPTER ELEVEN

THE IRRITATION OF BETRAYAL

FOR JESUS, THE MOST painful expression of self-will that He endured from another was the betrayal of Judas. He was an agent sent by the devil to betray Jesus into the perfect will of God. This denial did not catch Jesus by surprise, for He had said earlier:

Have not I chosen you twelve, and one of you is a devil? (John 6:70).

During the three and a half years that Jesus ministered to and with His disciples, there was never an indication that Judas was not totally submitted to the will of Jesus. He acted as treasurer for the group; he fed the multitude with the others and even joined them in their ministry as they were sent out two by two. It is possible, however, that he gave this submission with reservation. It is likely that he had his eyes on a position in an earthly, political kingdom and was willing to do anything necessary to achieve this position. Many think his betrayal was a desperate attempt to force Jesus to rise up against the existing political structure and become the king of Israel.

If this is true, his submission was deceitful. He was working to gain his own end. This is common to human nature. Marriage partners will submit to one another only as part of a scheme of manipulation to gain their own way. Business partners often declare similar goals and wills until such a time as they feel they can take over completely.

Jesus was always aware of the deceitfulness of Judas. Although He knew what Judas had planned, He graciously granted Judas permission to leave the upper room to go on his mission of betrayal. John, an eyewitness, tells us:

> And after the sop Satan entered into him.
> Then said Jesus unto him, That thou doest, do
> quickly (John 13:27).

Even though Jesus knew this coming betrayal was the work of Satan, it was a painful irritant to have it come through one whom He had called, trained and trusted. As the psalmist before Him had said:

> Yea, mine own familiar friend, in whom I
> trusted, which did eat of my bread, hath lifted
> up his heel against me (Psalm 41:9).

In this psalm David was probably referring to the insurrection of his son Absalom, but the Holy Spirit was looking forward to Judas. In both cases the betrayal was done with outward sweetness but deceitful motives. When Judas finally brought the religious officers to the garden to turn Christ over to their guards, Jesus was talking to His disciples after an agonizing time of prayer.

> And while he yet spake, behold a multitude, and he that was called Judas, one of the twelve, went before them, and drew near unto Jesus to kiss him. But Jesus said unto him, Judas, betrayest thou the Son of man with a kiss? (Luke 22:47-48).

Little wonder, then, that we have coined the phrase, "Betrayed with a kiss." Every one of us can probably think of an incident where someone in whom we invested time and effort betrayed our confidence.

When I began Scottsdale Worship Center, a young man approached me expressing a deep longing to be in the ministry. "Let me join you and work as your associate," he pled.

We were far too young and small to afford a staff member, but he was so insistent that I agreed to use him as a youth director but told him that he would have to work to support himself until the church was financially strong enough to take him on full-time.

It soon became obvious to me that he lacked the initiative to be a leader, but he did have a fair capacity for leading in worship, so I made him my song leader and worship director. I poured into him everything I had learned over the years. He needed guidance in handling his financial affairs and required much counseling to put his home in order. For the first two years he was really more trouble than he was worth, but he was learning. When I began to feel that my labor was paying off, he walked into my office one morning and told me that his employer had offered to underwrite the expenses of starting a new church. He told me the date of his first service and asked for my blessing.

I did everything in my power to convince him that he was not ready for the responsibilities of pastoring. I pointed out that he still lacked the leadership qualities needed to start a church, but he would not listen. He did what I had done a few years earlier and rented a school building for Sunday mornings. He put an ad in the paper and talked to our church members about his "call." He took as many members of my congregation as would go with him, and as long as his employer would pay the bills, he had his church on Sunday morning.

The predictable happened. The new work died of spiritual anemia. His betrayal of my trust and time investment in him had hurt our small congregation. Those who went with him became disillusioned and never returned. They have joined the ranks of wounded Christians everywhere. The young man is out of the ministry, spiritually injured by self-inflicted wounds.

When he made his break from us, we chose to bless him rather than withstand him. Our congregation prayed for him and for his fledgling church on his final Sunday with us and on succeeding Sundays. Although the church he tried to birth didn't survive its infancy, I now realize that my church's refusal to make a battle out of this betrayal formed a protective sac into which we poured the nacre of love and concern that formed a pearl. This took the edge off the pain and left us with a valuable jewel after this experience was over.

Jesus knew Judas would betray Him, but He still trained him, used him and even trusted him with the treasury. Jesus chose to cover this painful irritant with love instead of expelling it with distrust and penalty. He even made it easy for Judas to fulfill his scheme of betrayal by dismissing him from the upper room.

Each of us needs to be on guard lest betrayal by one

makes us unduly suspicious of all. A woman whose husband leaves her for another woman can easily become suspicious of all men. Yet, betrayed or not, we need to be realistic enough to know that not everyone into whom we pour our lives will remain trustworthy, for each of us has a free will and all the self-centeredness that comes with it.

When Paul headed for Jerusalem, which eventually took him to Rome and martyrdom, he met with the elders into whom he had deposited so much of himself. Amidst their weeping and sorrow over his testimony that he would probably never see them again, Paul said:

> For I know this, that after my departing shall grievous wolves enter in among you, not sparing the flock. Also of your own selves shall men arise, speaking perverse things, to draw away disciples after them (Acts 20:29-30).

Paul knew their self-wills would cause dissension among them and produce friction once he was off the scene. Although Paul taught them wisely and trusted them implicitly, he was a realist. He knew their human nature would override their spiritual desires on some future occasion. But in spite of this knowledge, Paul loved and blessed each of them. With what was facing him in Jerusalem, the last thing Paul needed was a root of bitterness in his spirit.

What is true in the religious world is also true in the natural world. Children often throw aside years of training, love, provision and prayers in the exercise of their own wills. Parents are despised and often mistreated. Some are robbed, either by outright theft or by loans that are never repaid. Others are more viciously declared incompetent and put in institutions so their assets can be squandered.

Betrayal comes in many different packages. Those who work with our legal system know that the danger of plea bargaining is the potential of betrayal in the final moments, and there is no recourse. Betrayal in business dealings is so common as to nearly underwrite the careers of lawyers. Close friends betray confidences and employees betray trade secrets. Betrayal in marriage is so common that marriages now have less than a fifty percent chance of succeeding.

There is probably no way to prevent being betrayed somewhere and in some way during your lifetime. It will hurt. It may be very destructive, but it need not be deadly. Learn to make a pearl out of this intruding grain of sand. Contain the irritant where it enters. Don't let it get to your spirit — keep it in the physical and emotional realm. Then pour the love of Christ all over it. Rest in the assurance that the Lord will never betray you, and know that His love undergirds you in the midst of another's betrayal.

Every attempt on your part to get vengeance on your betrayer will only wound you more deeply than the betrayer wounded you. If there is a lesson to be learned, learn it, but don't try to "teach him or her a lesson." Make a pearl; don't create a predicament.

Perhaps the measure of pain that betrayal inflicts is in direct proportion to the level of expectation we had in the betrayer. The higher our expectations are in another, the deeper the wound when they betray us. Just as Jesus never violated the free moral agency of people, although it would have prevented betrayal, neither should we. Often our betrayal is far less a rejection of ourselves than it is an elevating of the betrayer. The heart of their betrayal is the exercise of their self-will, no matter how painful it may be to others.

Selfishness and greed usually form the basis for betrayal. If there is nothing in it for the betrayer, it is unlikely he or she would enter into betrayal. Even Judas got thirty pieces of silver for betraying Jesus.

Insurrection and betrayal seem to be part of life. It is certainly par for the course in leadership. Moses experienced it in the uprising of Korah, who declared that Moses had taken too much authority upon himself and that the leadership should be shared with others, especially Korah and his followers.

David experienced the pain of betrayal and insurrection from his son Absalom. Absalom set forth to win the hearts of key people in Israel and finally dared to declare himself king in his father's place. He drove his father from Jerusalem to the wilderness and took over the palace and the kingdom. It was an experience David had great difficulty living through. Christian parents still experience the betrayal of their children in spite of all they have poured into them.

Jesus experienced betrayal from Judas, and Paul anticipated it in his elders. Christians still experience it. Employees often come to the end of years of service to find they have been betrayed in their retirement funds. Voters are often betrayed by those who were elected to an office — they promise one thing and do the opposite once they take over their official duties.

Betrayal is part of life because the selfish human nature with which we are born is often willing to do anything necessary to obtain personal goals and ambitions. Such betrayal makes some people bitter and it makes others better. Some spend the rest of their lives talking about their deep pain, while others cover this irritant with the love of Christ and form a pearl.

As we learn from Marvin the oyster, the pearl is not

produced by the foreign substance that enters the mantle, but by what the oyster does with it. Only mollusks that are lined with mother-of-pearl produce the really fine pearls. The lining is the same material the oyster secretes to build up concentrated layers of pearl around the irritant.

Jesus produced ultra-fine pearls because His life was lined with the very substance from which pearls are formed. He did not merely have a measure of love that could be secreted around irritants, but His entire life was lined with God's love. He merely covered these irritants with His very nature.

Christian believers need to have their lives lined with the forgiving love of Jesus. We have received it. We should live in its presence. This will enable us to produce really fine pearls characterized by translucence and luster and by a delicate play of surface color that jewelers call *orient*. Pearls of this quality come from oysters whose insides are lined with the very substance of which pearls are formed. Perhaps this concept is included in Paul's statement:

> ...Christ in you, the hope of glory (Colossians 1:27).

All beauty, all glory and everything of value that will ever come from within us will be the result of the indwelling Christ. Even when our lives are lined with love, we often encounter abuse that we don't deserve. The next chapter shows us how to handle this abuse by looking at the most abusive day in the life of Jesus. O

CHAPTER TWELVE

THE IRRITATION OF UNDESERVED ABUSE

I WENT TO HIGH SCHOOL in Bandon, Oregon, a lumber town situated at the mouth of the Coquille River where it meets the Pacific Ocean. Playing on the beach was a favorite pastime, and scavenging along the beach after a major storm was often quite profitable. Scrounging amid the flotsam that had washed ashore, we sometimes found the glass balls used by Japanese fishing fleets to secure their nets. The balls often spent years floating in the ocean after they broke free from a net. It took a major storm to blow them out of the Japanese current that was several miles off the Oregon coast. Such a find was always a bonanza, for the tourists paid good prices for these glass floats.

The force of the waves during a storm also broke mollusks free from their grip on the rocks and washed them onto the beaches. The sea gulls would enjoy a feast the next day. A gull would swoop down and grasp a mollusk in its beak and then fly two or three hundred feet above a rock and drop the mollusk. The gull immediately glided down to the rock to see if the fall had broken the shell open enough to allow the bird to feast on the contents. If not, the gull repeated the operation. I used to wonder how that defenseless mollusk felt in being swept up into the air and then repeatedly dropped onto a hard surface. Wasn't it punishment enough to be dislodged from its home without being tortured by a bird that wanted to eat it?

Sometimes when I read the account of the crucifixion of Jesus, I think of this scene on the Bandon beach. The cruelty inflicted upon Jesus speaks loudly of the depravity of sinful human nature. It was as though person after person swept down, lifted Jesus to heights, and then dropped Him onto a rock, seeking to break Him open for the kill. It appears to me that in twenty-four hours Jesus suffered every form of abuse that is common to humanity.

The final hours of Christ's life on earth were filled with *emotional abuse*. This began at the Mount of Olives. The unwillingness or inability of Peter, James and John to pray with Him in Gethsemane added deeply to His emotional distress during these hours. The inner conflict was severe enough that Dr. Luke tells us:

> And being in an agony he prayed more earnestly: and his sweat was as it were great drops of blood falling down to the ground (Luke 22:44).

The lack of sensitivity by the three disciples who formed the inner circle around Jesus added to His emotional anguish. It seemed that no one cared what He was going through.

Jesus rebuked these disciples, but before He could explain the seriousness of the situation, Judas arrived with the soldiers and gave Jesus the kiss of betrayal. While Jesus expected this, it still came as an emotional blow. It didn't help matters any when clumsy Peter whipped out a sword and cut off the ear of a servant to the high priest. Instead of getting emotional support, Jesus found Himself once again rescuing a disciple from himself. Jesus compassionately reached through His emotional pain to heal that wounded ear — lest the high priest arrest Peter also.

As the soldiers bound the hands of Jesus behind Him before leading Him away, the Lord saw disciple after disciple slip into the darkness of the night and run for his life. Not only was He betrayed — He was also abandoned. Only John and Peter remained within the light of the torches.

Because they did not know how to handle their own emotional needs, the disciples failed to be supportive of Jesus. Instead, they contributed to His emotional distress. Their insensitivity, betrayal, misdirected activity and abandonment only proved how self-serving they actually were. Jesus learned what many since have discovered: Those closest to us inflict the deepest emotional wounds.

When Jesus was securely in the hands of His enemies, they began to inflict every possible emotional wound. During the mock trial before the hastily summoned Sanhedrin at the home of Caiaphas, the high priest, Jesus cringed inwardly as carefully coached false witnesses told lie after lie. Jesus lacked a defender, and the high priest admitted nothing Jesus said as evidence. Jesus knew that they would declare Him guilty because of their anger, not because of His actions. Outside of the high priest's home, Peter denied any association with Him at all.

It was similar when they took Jesus to Pontius Pilate

in the morning hours. The questioning there touched deep sensitive issues in the heart of Jesus. The silence of Jesus convinced Pilate of Christ's innocence, but the Jewish leaders wouldn't accept this Roman governor's decision. When Pilate sought to release Jesus as the pardoned prisoner he was required to free on the feast day, the crowd of people gathered outside demanded the release of Barabbas instead of Jesus.

First, Jesus was deserted by His disciples, and then the very people to whom He had ministered turned against Him. It cut deeply into His soul. This emotional abuse came from His professed friends. The prophet declared rightly:

> And one shall say unto him, What are these wounds in thine hands? Then he shall answer, Those with which I was wounded in the house of my friends (Zechariah 13:6).

The insults, challenges, mockeries and accusations hurled at Jesus when Pilate sent him to Herod only increased the emotional and mental abuse Jesus suffered on His way to Calvary. Later, when He tried to carry His cross down the streets of Jerusalem, the multitude taunted, jeered and laughed at Him. Even when He was hanging on the cruel Roman cross, one of the criminals crucified alongside of Him mocked Jesus and challenged Him to prove that He was who He said He was.

Emotional abuse is cumulative. Jesus lacked time to purge Himself from this abuse, for it came in rapid-fire succession. While He was still struggling with this mental and emotional abuse, the *physical abuse* began.

When Pilate saw that he could not release Jesus without creating a major disturbance among the crowd, he handed Jesus over to the soldiers for crucifixion. They did not immediately impale Jesus on a cross. Instead, they scourged Jesus with the cruel Roman cat-o'-nine-tails. Thirty-nine times those leather cords imbedded with glass and metal tore across the back of Jesus. Matthew says:

> Then the soldiers of the governor took Jesus into the common hall, and gathered unto him the whole band of soldiers. And they stripped him, and put on him a scarlet robe. And when they had plaited a crown of thorns, they put it upon his head, and a reed in his right hand: and they bowed the knee before him, and mocked him, saying, Hail, King of the Jews! And they spit upon him, and took the reed, and smote him on the head (Matthew 27:27-30).

Jesus was in the hands of executioners to whom torture was a game. Secular descriptions of Roman crucifixions are far more graphic than biblical accounts. The men who were assigned to carry out a crucifixion would often form a betting pool. Contributors gained the right to a single punch at the condemned man, and the entire sum of money went to the soldier whose punch killed him. You can believe that these men were well practiced in the art of killing.

Though they did not succeed in killing Jesus, the beating at the whipping post and the battering He took in the common hall so weakened Jesus that the soldiers had to compel Simon of Cyrene to carry the cross behind Jesus.

In looking forward with the vision of a seer, Isaiah saw the physical condition of Jesus as He was led to Calvary. He wrote:

> For he shall grow up before him as a tender
> plant, and as a root out of a dry ground: he
> hath no form nor comeliness; and when we
> shall see him, there is no beauty that we
> should desire him. He is despised and re-
> jected of men; a man of sorrows, and ac-
> quainted with grief: and we hid as it were our
> faces from him; he was despised, and we es-
> teemed him not (Isaiah 53:2-3).

The thrust of the Hebrew language is that the soldiers
so battered and mangled Jesus that He didn't even look
like a man. Bruised, buffeted, butchered and bleeding,
He looked like the soldiers had just pulled Him out of a
riot. The poison from the crown of thorns and the
pounding of the soldiers produced great swelling and
pain. Hair had been yanked from Christ's head and
beard, leaving open wounds in the scalp and cheeks, for
we read:

> I gave my back to the smiters, and my cheeks
> to them that plucked off the hair: I hid not my
> face from shame and spitting (Isaiah 50:6).

Pilate had not authorized the torture the soldiers inflicted on Jesus. He had sentenced Christ to crucifixion.
This torture was an improvisation that grew out of the
soldiers' frustrations. They made Jesus a victim of their
misdirected anger.

Jesus not only suffered emotional and physical abuse
before His crucifixion, but the soldiers also subjected
Him to sexual abuse. At the common hall, the soldiers
stripped Him in front of the entire guard. Later, when
He hung on the cross, the soldiers pulled his garment
from Him and gambled to see who could keep it. Jesus

was completely exposed in front of everyone. It was an embarrassing, degrading, moral abuse of an order higher than our permissive society can understand.

The act of crucifixion was physically punishing enough without all this painful abuse. The pounding of the spikes through the hands and feet (more likely the wrists and ankles) was just the beginning of the ordeal. When they lifted the cross to the vertical position and dropped it into the hole in the ground, the body jolted downward; dislocating the shoulders and often the elbows. After a while the muscles cramped violently and breathing became possible only by pushing up from the feet. Death by crucifixion was very slow and painful. Victims often lingered several days before finally dying. This is why Pilate marvelled that Jesus died so quickly (see Mark 15:44).

The overwhelming thing about Jesus' suffering was that it was all undeserved. The entire New Testament teaches that Jesus died as a fulfillment of the sacrifice on the Day of Atonement. He was the substitutionary lamb offered for the sins of the people.

The provision of the law was clear. This lamb was to be spotless and without blemish. The priests separated it from the flock for fourteen days and inspected it before offering it. The lamb could not have any disease or infirmity. Jesus met this prerequisite by being set apart for three years. During that time, He proved to be sinless and without stain, but when it came time for Him to be offered, He was treated much differently than they had ever treated any Old Testament sacrifice.

The Old Testament sacrifices were slain as mercifully as possible. They did not beat the animal, nor did they humiliate, tease or debase it. The animal was their substitute, and they treated it with dignity. Yet beatings, humiliation and debasement preceded the death of Jesus. He who became our Paschal Lamb was severely abused before He could offer Himself unto God.

A current buzzword of our generation is *abuse*. Stories of abuse that have long been hidden are now openly discussed in public forums and in the press. Pastors find themselves inundated with people pouring out their long-repressed resentment and anger at having been molested, abused and neglected in their childhood days. Psychologists tell us that these unresolved experiences deeply affect the personalities of the abused.

I have cringed inwardly as I have listened to members of my congregation tell of sexual abuse that they endured in their childhood. Fathers have used their daughters to gratify their sexual urges without realizing what permanent damage they were inflicting on them. Not only do these daughters grow up resenting men, but they also often take offense at all authority figures. Worse than this, they usually find it almost impossible to relate lovingly to God, for they see God as a father like they had. After all, didn't Jesus teach us to pray, "Our Father which art in heaven..."?

It's also not pleasant to admit how much time I've spent listening to men and women graphically recount the repeated physical abuse they endured while growing up. Their parents directed their anger at the children. They tell of repeated beatings, of being tied up or locked in a room for days on end. Some speak of being tortured with fire or cigarettes, while others were deprived of necessary food and water.

Other adults speak of having to endure severe emotional abuse. Their parents continually told them they were worthless. They cursed, criticized and mocked them. The father teased them, and the mother ridiculed them while the brothers and sisters demoralized them whenever possible.

It doesn't seem to matter whether the abuse was emotional, physical or sexual. The pain goes on and sometimes the afflicted become the afflictors. Because they never learned how to channel anger and frustration properly, they do to their children what was done to them. Abuse is a vicious cycle.

Why did God the Father allow His Son, Jesus, to endure this serious irritation of undeserved abuse? Namely because He could then become an example for us. While on the cross, He prayed:

> Father, forgive them; for they know not what
> they do (Luke 23:34).

One thing I hear repeatedly in the counseling chambers is, "I didn't know anyone else ever experienced this." Now that the shame of abuse is coming into the open, abuse support groups are gathering to help people share experiences and draw strength from one another.

But as Christians we can't honestly say, "No one has ever gone through what I have gone through." Jesus suffered extreme abuse long before we were born. The writer to the Hebrew Christians says:

> For we have not an high priest which cannot
> be touched with the feeling of our infirmities;
> but was in all points tempted like as we are,
> yet without sin (Hebrews 4:15).

Jesus not only bore our sins, He took our sufferings as well. He thoroughly understands undeserved abuse. He knows the defenseless position of children. He understands the helpless situation of the beaten wife. He knows what it is like to become the object of undeserved anger unleashed in great frustration. He endured and suffered it, and He can identify with us in it. The prophet assured us:

> Surely he hath borne our griefs, and carried our sorrows: yet we did esteem him stricken, smitten of God, and afflicted (Isaiah 53:4).

Knowing Jesus was also abused may not take away your pain, but it should make talking it over with Him much easier and more meaningful. He can verify your feelings by checking them against His own feelings. It is never out of order to discuss your feelings with Jesus. Paul urges us:

> Be careful for [anxious about] nothing; but in every thing by prayer and supplication with thanksgiving let your requests be made known unto God (Philippians 4:6).

When you discuss your abuse with Jesus, you have a far more understanding listener than you will find in an abuse support group.

Jesus not only experienced abuse so He could verify ours through identification, but He accepted undeserved abuse as a substitute for us. Just as He vicariously bore our sins, isn't it likely that Jesus equally bore this abuse on our behalf? After telling us that Jesus did indeed bear grief and sorrow Isaiah adds:

> But he was wounded for our transgressions, he was bruised for our iniquities: the chastisement of our peace was upon him; and with his stripes we are healed (Isaiah 53:5).

He was wounded, bruised and chastised on our behalf. He died to save us from sin. He shared in our wounds and bruises to save us from their destructive power as well. We need not bear something that He has already borne for us. Just as we roll our sins onto Him, we can roll our abuses onto Him as well.

In the Old Testament when the priest slew a sacrificial animal, he caught the blood in a basin. He then sprinkled some of that blood on the garments of the sacrificer, and then he poured the remainder at the base of the altar. The letter to the Hebrew Christians affirms:

> Let us draw near with a true heart in full assurance of faith, having our hearts sprinkled from an evil conscience, and our bodies washed with pure water (Hebrews 10:22).

As a student of the Old Testament types, I think that the sprinkling of the blood dealt with the inner conscience or memory.

The Weymouth New Testament translates this, "...hearts sprinkled clean from consciences oppressed with sin." Similarly, the Twentieth Century New Testament translates it, "Having our hearts purified by the sprinkled blood from all consciousness of wrong." The blood of Jesus is an identification with our hurts. He was wounded to the point of bleeding, and when we sprinkle that blood by faith it purifies our inner person from all consciousness of sin and its accompanying guilt. God's Word declares to us:

> If we say that we have no sin, we deceive ourselves, and the truth is not in us. If we confess our sins, he is faithful and just to forgive us our sins, and to cleanse us from all unrighteousness (1 John 1:8-9).

A life that confesses sin becomes a life cleansed from sin.

No matter how serious the wrong we have done, God forgives us, removes the penalty and cleanses our consciences.

The sprinkled blood also purifies our consciousness of wrong done to us. Often when another has wronged us, the offense hangs in our conscious mind far longer than when we have wronged someone else. Abuse is a valid case in point. Long after the abuser is dead and buried, the pain he or she inflicted stays in our consciences, unless we bring it to the blood of Jesus for a complete cleansing. Jesus suffered to the point of shedding blood to cleanse our hearts from the pain of past sufferings.

The sprinkled blood also purges our consciences from the guilt that we feel when others make false judgments about us. When a person is consistently told he or she is worthless or inept, it leaves a deep impression on the mind. That memory will hinder and infect us throughout our adult lives unless it is confronted and removed. Jesus was slandered, maligned and even called an agent of Satan in order to cleanse our minds from the false projections made to us.

While it is true that a series of counseling sessions with a trained professional can often rid us of these feelings of guilt and the pain of abuse, Jesus has made full provision to do this at Calvary. We simply need to apply the blood of Calvary to our wounds, hurts and bitternesses. Jesus bore these hurts so that He could relieve us from having to bear them. We need to openly expose them to Him in prayer and allow the same forgiving grace that formed a pearl in Him to bring a healing balm in us that will further protect us during our time here on earth.

If Jesus could forgive those who abused Him, His life in us can still help us forgive those who have abused us. We have tried to forgive them with our own grace, but it has not been sufficient. We need to allow the Christ within us to say:

> Father, forgive them; for they know not what they do (Luke 23:34).

He shed His blood while undergoing abuse to make it possible for us to be able to pray for our abusers. Now we need to learn to sprinkle that blood in our own lives.

It is the application of the blood of Jesus to our many abuses that can form a pearl out of these damaging irritants. The applied blood of Jesus will also cover the sins that we commit ourselves. In fact, as Jesus identified with our sin, he felt the most crushing irritation of His entire life. Our final lesson from the Pearlmaker focuses on the irritation of vicarious sin. O

CHAPTER THIRTEEN

THE IRRITATION OF VICARIOUS SIN

OF ALL THE IRRITANTS that slipped into the life of Jesus when He was on earth, nothing came close to producing the pain that was spawned by sin. The torment the executioners inflicted upon Jesus was nothing compared to the trouble His Father imposed upon Him. The high priest and the Sanhedrin initiated internal misery to Christ's soul. The Roman soldiers inflicted external torture to His body, but the heavenly Father induced intense sorrow to His Son's spirit.

All this hurtful humiliation was cumulative and progressive, and it came upon Jesus within the space of a few hours. The physical pain He suffered was the least of His sorrows. The psalmist spoke prophetically of an inner affliction that far exceeded the outer:

> Therefore is my spirit overwhelmed within me; my heart within me is desolate (Psalm 143:4).

Jesus had entered Jerusalem on a donkey just a week earlier. The multitude of people waved palm fronds and threw their garments on the road in front of Jesus, forming an impromptu triumphal procession. Mark quotes Peter, who was part of the processional, as saying:

> And they that went before, and they that followed, cried, saying, Hosanna; Blessed is he that cometh in the name of the Lord: Blessed be the kingdom of our father David, that cometh in the name of the Lord: Hosanna in the highest (Mark 11:9-10).

Now a week later Jesus again marches through Jerusalem, but the reaction of this crowd is entirely different. They didn't see a conqueror riding into the city to overthrow the Roman government. They saw a beaten, mangled man whom the Romans had condemned to death by crucifixion. As the prophet described Jesus:

> He is despised and rejected of men; a man of sorrows, and acquainted with grief: and we hid as it were our faces from him; he was despised, and we esteemed him not (Isaiah 53:3).

What an amazing change of events can occur in a week's time. Their champion had become a criminal in their eyes, but the fickleness of the multitude was not what hurt Jesus. Nor was it the total injustice of everything that was happening. His Spirit was crushed by the sudden awareness of sin.

Jesus, conceived of the Holy Spirit and born of a virgin, came into this world as sinless as God had created Adam and Eve. His initial mission was to see if

God was responsible for man's sin. Jesus became a "test model" to search for flaws in that original creation. Jesus lived on this earth for thirty-three years but without the sinless surroundings that Adam enjoyed in the garden. Jesus was repeatedly tempted to sin, but He remained sinless. In doing so, He proved that Adam's sin was not the result of a flaw in the creation of humanity. It was an act of Adam's will. After the ascension of Jesus, the Holy Spirit wrote:

> For we have not an high priest which cannot
> be touched with the feeling of our infirmities;
> but was in all points tempted like as we are,
> yet without sin (Hebrews 4:15).

Jesus successfully resisted the seducing power of every sin that pressed upon His life.

During His ministry on earth Jesus dealt with sin in the lives of others, constantly working against sin's products and effects. He exercised authority over the arch-sinner, Satan, and He showed abundant mercy to those people who were trapped in the clutches of sin. He was also aware of the side effects of sin, for His own people were oppressed subjects of the Roman empire and were virtual slaves to the poverty and oppression that usually accompany the reign of sin.

All this sin remained outside Jesus. He could see sin, but He did not feel it. He knew its effects, but He did not know its power from experience. It would be similar to me sitting in my air-conditioned office in Phoenix and looking through the window at people outside in the blistering heat of a summer day. Intellectually, I know they are hot, but I don't feel what they feel.

At some time during the maltreatment that surrounded Christ's crucifixion, God the Father laid on His only begotten Son the sin of the whole world. The prophet foretold this event:

> All we like sheep have gone astray; we have turned every one to his own way; and the Lord hath laid on him the iniquity of us all (Isaiah 53:6).

It would have been severe enough had Jesus committed just a single personal sin — even in His thought life — but God laid on Jesus the weight of every sin — from Satan's insurrection in heaven to the present inhumanity of the crucifixion. All sin was heaped on Him in the same instant.

We are born in sin, and the weight of personal sin becomes cumulative. Like the donkey whose back is laden down with one item at a time, we learn to adjust to the weight of sin. But God instantly dropped the full load of the world's sin on Jesus. He didn't have years to get used to the weight of sin. He went from sinlessness to sinfulness in a moment's time. How God the Father did this is as difficult to understand as the virgin birth of Jesus. God does not attempt to explain His methods. He merely tells us His mission.

Jesus had never before experienced the emotions of sin. They were as foreign to His nature as sight is to a person who is born blind. When the weight of sin fell on Jesus, He who had testified that He delighted to do His Father's will suddenly felt the repulsive rebellion that sin induces. The frustrating fury that began to burn deep within Him completely overwhelmed Him. He became confused at the physical passions that now screamed for satisfaction, for these had previously been under perfect control in His life. He also sensed an invisible wall rising up between Himself and the Father, a wall that separated Him so completely from the absolute oneness He had always shared with God that on the cross He cried:

> My God, my God, why hast thou forsaken me? why art thou so far from helping me, and from the words of my roaring? (Psalm 22:1; also see Mark 15:34).

Jesus was experiencing the complete separation from God that sin produces. The depth of His anguish increased in the knowledge that none of this sin was the result of His personal action. It was all our sin. His work was vicarious.

As severe as this was, the worst was yet to come. God the Father did more than just lay all our sins on Jesus — He caused Jesus to become sin. The Bible declares:

> For he hath made him to be sin for us, who knew no sin; that we might be made the right-eousness of God in him (2 Corinthians 5:21).

The New King James Version translation puts it: "For He made Him who knew no sin to be sin for us...." Jesus became sin — whatever that repugnant, repulsive thing is. We mere humans do not understand the true nature of sin. We see only its evidence and effect. We perceive something of sin's presence and power, but we do not understand its personality. We know sin as an attitude or an act. Jesus knew sin as a living principle.

In this verse in 2 Corinthians, Paul pits sin as the antonym of righteousness. Whatever righteousness is not, sin is. Jesus, whom the Bible declares to be the "righteous servant" (Isaiah 53:11), became the exact opposite of righteousness by an action of His Father. It was a total change of nature for Jesus. The contrast was as great as a man being transformed into a dog.

Why? Jesus had completely surrendered to the perfect will of God the Father in the Garden of Gethsemane. He was headed to Calvary to pay the penalty for sin, though He had proved that the Godhead was not responsible for the sin problem. Jesus had lived an absolutely sinless life in surroundings far more oppressive and tempting than Adam and Eve ever faced. What was God's purpose in making Jesus not only become the sin bearer, but sin itself?

The answer to that question was written by the prophet Isaiah thousands of years ago:

> Surely he hath borne our griefs, and carried our sorrows: yet we did esteem him stricken, smitten of God, and afflicted. But he was wounded for our transgressions, he was bruised for our iniquities: the chastisement of our peace was upon him; and with his stripes we are healed (Isaiah 53:4-5).

None of this sin was His. All of it was ours. Jesus became our substitute, as surely as the Old Testament lamb was a substitute for the one sacrificing it. The entire sacrificial system was a vicarious one. It substituted the innocent for the guilty.

We sometimes forget that the Old Testament provision of atonement through sacrifice required more than the death of an animal. It demanded an identification with that death. The worshipper needed to understand the death of the sacrificial animal as substitutionary. He laid his hands on the animal while it still lived and confessed his sins in the presence of the priest. By identification he put his personal sins on the animal. When the animal died, the Israelite visualized himself as dying —

paying the penalty — for his sins. He accepted that the penalty for his sins had been satisfied and that his sins had been removed from his life.

God provided for an annual demonstration of this to the Israelites in the offering of the scapegoat (see Leviticus 16). The priests arbitrarily chose two goats as sin offerings for the entire nation. The priests confessed the national sins over the goats and then cast lots over them to choose the scapegoat. A selected person then led this goat into the wilderness and released it. Israel visualized the scapegoat as the sin bearer that took away the sins of the nation. Then the priests sacrificed the other goat to satisfy the just claims of the law.

Jesus came to pay the penalty of death for our sins. He also bore those sins in His body. Like the scapegoat, He took those sins away from us so we need never bear them again. His death satisfied the just claims of the law of God, but when He took our sins into His life and carried them to Calvary, He released us from the presence, power and pollution of sin once and forever. Hallelujah! Paul put it this way:

> For he hath made him to be sin for us, who knew no sin; that we might be made the righteousness of God in him (2 Corinthians 5:21).

God made Jesus to be unrighteous to make us righteous. Jesus became sin so He could make us to become sinless. In bearing the power of sin at Calvary, Jesus broke the power of sin in our lives. Because of His vicarious sin-bearing, Jesus can assure us:

> For sin shall not have dominion over you: for ye are not under the law, but under grace (Romans 6:14).

Nothing that Jesus bore at Calvary need be borne by us in this life. As Peter expressed it:

> Who his own self bare our sins in his own body on the tree, that we, being dead to sins, should live unto righteousness: by whose stripes ye were healed (1 Peter 2:24).

Jesus became sin that we might become saints. He suffered hurts that we might be healed. He died that we might live. It was a trade-off, but it was a very unfair exchange. It cost heaven God's only Son just to rescue hell-bound sinners. No businessman would consider this a profitable business arrangement, but God had a love motive, not a profit motive. We read:

> But God commendeth his love toward us, in that, while we were yet sinners, Christ died for us (Romans 5:8).

This irritant of vicarious sin-bearing was worse than all the other irritants of His life. Was the price for this pearl too high? We are unable to calculate the severity of the trouble that caused Jesus to flow the nacre of divine love to form this pearl of great price, which could not be extracted without killing Jesus. But that was true of Marvin the oyster, wasn't it? Until the knife of the oyster shucker cuts the muscle that holds the two shells together, the pearl cannot be found. Likewise, it took the death of Jesus on the cross to reveal the beautiful, spiritual pearls that He had been forming throughout His life on earth.

In all His sufferings, Jesus refused to blame the devil. He dealt exclusively with God the Father. He came in God's will with the declared purpose of doing God's will. He was aware of Satan's resistance, but Jesus did little more than rebuke him with the Word of God.

Jesus recognized that trouble does not accomplish its purpose if we doubt God's character or interpret that trouble as His dissatisfaction. Jesus knew that trouble does not mean we have missed God's will, for it is often part of that divine will. Jesus consistently accepted induced irritants as part of God's will for His life, but He formed pearls around them.

Jesus unwaveringly refused to fall into depression because of these irritants. He knew, better than we do, that depression breeds deception. He was never deceived about His mission or the method God had chosen for its completion. Instead of succumbing to self-pity, Jesus kept a joyful attitude. We read:

> Looking unto Jesus the author and finisher of our faith; who for the joy that was set before him endured the cross, despising the shame, and is set down at the right hand of the throne of God (Hebrews 12:2).

He didn't focus on the trouble that seemed to be perpetually on the horizon. Jesus focused on the joy that God had set in front of Him. He learned to handle trouble joyfully and became a pearlmaker.

We need to look to Jesus repeatedly as the pattern for handling life's irritants, even the irritant of personal sin. While we never can bear the sins of another, we do frequently carry personal sins in our lives. These are deadly. Harboring sin is one irritant that we cannot cover, and it must be removed. God has provided the sacrificial blood of Jesus Christ to remove that irritating sin from our lives. The promise is:

> The blood of Jesus Christ his Son cleanseth
> us from all sin. If we say that we have no sin,
> we deceive ourselves, and the truth is not in
> us. If we confess our sins, he is faithful and
> just to forgive us our sins, and to cleanse us
> from all unrighteousness (1 John 1:7-9).

The worst thing any of us can do is try to cover our
sins. God has no desire to make something beautiful out
of sin.

Cleansing, not covering, is God's provision for personal sin. In fact, the Bible warns us:

> He that covereth his sins shall not prosper:
> but whoso confesseth and forsaketh them
> shall have mercy (Proverbs 28:13).

Remember the scapegoat of Old Testament times?
Jesus has become our scapegoat. Through Him God has
provided for the complete removal of our sins. Christ's
crucifixion fully satisfied the penalty of death that the
law imposed upon sinners. His vicarious bearing of our
sins separated us from that sin permanently. David
graphically illustrated it by saying:

> As far as the east is from the west, so far hath
> he removed our transgressions from us
> (Psalm 103:12).

David was speaking from experience. He had not
only been forgiven, but his sins were so far removed
from him that he never repeated them, nor did God hold
them against him.

None of us can duplicate the sin-bearing ministry of
Jesus at Calvary. Instead, God invites us to identify with

the death of Jesus. Paul testified:

> I am crucified with Christ: nevertheless I
> live; yet not I, but Christ liveth in me: and the
> life which I now live in the flesh I live by the
> faith of the Son of God, who loved me, and
> gave himself for me (Galatians 2:20).

The beauty of the pearl that Jesus produced as our sin bearer is that He has done for us that which we cannot do. The death we deserved but could not survive is already behind us. Jesus died for us. Furthermore, the life we could not hope to attain became available to us in Christ's resurrection. We who were separated from God have been brought into an intimate relationship with Him through the blood of Jesus Christ. We have been made welcome into the family of God. Paul declared:

> According as he hath chosen us in him before
> the foundation of the world, that we should
> be holy and without blame before him in love
> (Ephesians 1:4).

God did not merely choose to redeem us. From the foundation of the world, He chose to restore us and enable us to be: 1) holy, 2) without blame, 3) in His presence and 4) in His love.

What beauty! What value! What glory! Christ brought the glorious pearl of redemption to humanity by suffering the disgrace of being made sin and by dying for that sin at Calvary.

This is the most valuable product of suffering that Jesus produced. None of the other products would benefit us without it. O

CHAPTER FOURTEEN

THE PRODUCT OF IRRITANTS

ONLY A MASOCHIST embraces suffering as pleasure. For the rest of us, we only bless trouble, pain and irritation in hindsight. The emotion produced by grief, misery and sorrow blocks out our philosophical view of life. When we are in the midst of affliction, we feel that life is, indeed, a bowl of cherries but we are in the pits.

This response to tribulation is not a product of living in the twentieth century. As far back as the days of the apostles, an inspired writer said:

> Now no chastening for the present seemeth to be joyous, but grievous: nevertheless afterward it yieldeth the peaceable fruit of righteousness unto them which are exercised thereby (Hebrews 12:11).

The key word in this verse is *afterward*. It is amazing how we have 20/20 vision in hindsight but are nearly blind when looking at our present situation. While undergoing the process of suffering irritants, we are unable to visualize the product, which is pearls.

In the past twelve chapters we have looked at various irritants that plagued Jesus during His three and a half years of ministry. We have suggested that the way He handled those irritations could have formed precious pearls represented by the twelve gates of the New Jerusalem. We have shown how those same irritants bother us, and that if we will allow the life of Jesus in us to cover those irritants with spiritual nacre, they will form beautiful pearls in us as well.

It would be unfair to end this book without looking, however briefly, at the New Jerusalem that has these twelve gorgeous gates of iridescent pearls. John, the revelator, describes this city in the final book of the Bible. He introduces us to the holy city by saying:

> And I saw a new heaven and a new earth: for the first heaven and the first earth were passed away; and there was no more sea. And I John saw the holy city, new Jerusalem, coming down from God out of heaven, prepared as a bride adorned for her husband (Revelation 21:1-2).

For centuries there has been a strong difference of opinion among Bible teachers about this city. Some believe, as Judson presents in his earlier book *Heaven*, that it is a literal city placed in orbit over the earth as the home of the glorified saints who will rule and reign over the renovated earth. Their position is that if verse one, which calls for a renovated earth, is literal, then verse two is equally as literal.

Others, such as my brother Robert, take a symbolic or

spiritual view of the city because John speaks of it as "a bride." They see the city as a metaphoric picture of the church. As the politician said of the issue of his day, "Some of my friends are for it. Some of my friends are against it. I stand with my friends."

I contentedly agree with my brother Judson, and, just as comfortably, I also agree with my brother Robert. I have no difficulty accommodating the apostle John's vision as both literal and spiritual, for the Old Testament abounds with natural events that foreshadow spiritual fulfillments. The apostle Paul often used events during Israel's wilderness wanderings to illustrate our walk with Christ. He even went as far as to affirm:

> Howbeit that was not first which is spiritual,
> but that which is natural; and afterward that
> which is spiritual (1 Corinthians 15:46).

Put in modern vernacular, Paul said: "First the natural, then the spiritual." Since we learn by proceeding from the known to the unknown, God mercifully demonstrates spiritual realities by natural means. Could not this be true with the New Jerusalem? Perhaps John described spiritual realities that are difficult to grasp in natural terms which we can more easily understand. John described the church as a city — the habitation of both God and the saints.

This idea of a specific location as the dwelling place of God is as ancient as the Bible itself. Noah's ark, the tabernacle in the wilderness, David's tabernacle and Solomon's temple are all examples of this imagery. They were places where men and women could approach the divine presence. God had set His name on each of these places, and on occasion His presence — the *shekinah* — rested on them. Still, none of them was the residence of God. They were merely places of God's visitation.

Each of these four places is a foreshadowing of the coming church. Noah's ark pictures the doctrines of the church. The tabernacle in the wilderness illustrates the function of the church. David's tabernacle pictures the heart of God among His people, and Solomon's temple speaks of the codified government of the coming church.

These were images of the coming church, but they were imperfect images. First, they were temporary. The first three didn't even have foundations. They were portable. Although Solomon built His temple for permanence, God let Nebuchadnezzar destroy it when the priests defiled it with idol worship.

This New Jerusalem, also called the holy city, has twelve massive gemstones for its foundation. God built it for permanence. God's church is not a temporary structure awaiting something greater. It is eternal. Paul says the church is:

> ...built upon the foundation of the apostles
> and prophets, Jesus Christ himself being the
> chief corner stone (Ephesians 2:20).

No wonder John saw it in eternity. The church has always been eternal in character.

The New Jerusalem is God's handiwork, a sharp contrast to the four dwelling places of God that were given in the Old Testament. Noah, with the help of his sons, built the ark to God's specifications. The tabernacle in the wilderness was built by the Israelites, although God gave an explicit pattern to follow.

Under the inspiration of the Holy Spirit, David designed and gathered all the necessary materials for the temple. Solomon, his son, built it. In contrast to these, it is the hand of Almighty God that builds the church. Jesus said:

> I say also unto thee, That thou art Peter, and upon this rock I will build my church; and the gates of hell shall not prevail against it (Matthew 16:18).

Furthermore, we read of Abraham:

> For he looked for a city which hath foundations, whose builder and maker is God (Hebrews 11:10).

A third strong contrast that shows how imperfect these Old Testament images were is that the church is pictured as the dwelling place of God, not just where He has placed His name and occasionally visits with His *shekinah*. John says of this holy city:

> The throne of God and of the Lamb shall be in it; and his servants shall serve him (Revelation 22:3). And he that sitteth on the throne shall dwell among them (Revelation 7:15).

God visited the places where men gathered to meet Him, but He inhabits His church. How out of order it is for us to seek a "visitation" of God's Spirit. God doesn't want to come as a visitor. He dwells among His people. He clearly declared:

> Know ye not that ye are the temple of God, and that the Spirit of God dwelleth in you? (1 Corinthians 3:16).

> And what agreement hath the temple of God
> with idols? for ye are the temple of the living
> God; as God hath said, I will dwell in them,
> and walk in them; and I will be their God,
> and they shall be my people (2 Corinthians
> 6:16).

The modern church does not need a revival of God's presence; it needs the residence of the presence of God. The New Jerusalem has this. If the holy city pictures the church, then God should be seen on the throne of His church on earth. It is His habitation and the residency of the saints. This habitation is built to last eternally. It has a sure foundation.

In contrasting the holy city with the cities of the earth, the things that could not be found in the New Jerusalem deeply impressed John. According to Revelation 21:4 and 22:3, it has:

1. No tears
2. No death
3. No sorrow
4. No crying
5. No pain
6. No curse

What a beautiful fulfillment of Christ's words from the cross: "It is finished" (John 19:30). The painful irritations of life will all be over. Only the pearls that these irritations forced us to form will remain. God's process is not eternal, but the product will remain throughout eternity.

If this city is literal, and it has only twelve gates, then only Jesus could have formed pearls massive enough to function as its entrances. However, if John's description of the city has a spiritual application, then there may be a sense in which the smaller pearls formed by the saints can also function as entrances to the throne of God. This possibility points to the dramatic differences in access to God in the Old and New Testaments.

In the Old Testament, each picture of God's habitation had but a single entrance. Noah's ark had but one door, for only Noah's family could enter. The tabernacle in the wilderness, David's tabernacle and Solomon's temple had only one gate to allow worshippers to enter, and the gate always faced to the east. Only God's covenant nation, Israel, worshipped there. But John was aware that the New Jerusalem has twelve entrances, very much like the twelve gates of ancient Jerusalem. These gates were divided equally among the four walls of this square city. Three gates faced each compass point.

Since the Old Testament deals primarily with the nation of Israel, God's covenant people, a single gate of entrance was fitting. Now, however, the promise of the New Testament is:

> For God so loved the world, that he gave his only begotten Son, that whosoever believeth in him should not perish, but have everlasting life (John 3:16).

God's localized habitation in the temple was basically for His covenant people — Israel. Still, His eternal plan had encompassed the entire world of humanity, for His promise to Abraham was:

> And thy seed shall be as the dust of the earth, and thou shalt spread abroad to the west, and to the east, and to the north, and to the south: and in thee and in thy seed shall all the families of the earth be blessed (Genesis 28:14).

The Product of Irritants

God's covenant love for Israel was extended to the world, as He had promised Abraham. This New Jerusalem is for the "whosoever will," and it needs three gates in each wall to accommodate the ingathering. It is not by accident that God spoke through His prophets and said:

> Fear not: for I am with thee: I will bring thy seed from the east, and gather thee from the west; I will say to the north, Give up; and to the south, Keep not back: bring my sons from far, and my daughters from the ends of the earth (Isaiah 43:5-6).

> But when the people of the land shall come before the Lord in the solemn feasts, he that entereth in by the way of the north gate to worship shall go out by the way of the south gate; and he that entereth by the way of the south gate shall go forth by the way of the north gate: he shall not return by the way of the gate whereby he came in, but shall go forth over against it (Ezekiel 46:9).

Jesus also told of people coming from all over the world to dwell in His presence:

> And they shall come from the east, and from the west, and from the north, and from the south, and shall sit down in the kingdom of God (Luke 13:29).

In the literal city, Jesus alone could form these gates. In the figure of the church, it is likely that we, the redeemed, function as routes of approach to God. The world does not see Christians as collective members constituting the church. The unbelievers view individuals as the church. To them, each believer represents God and becomes their entrance into the divine presence. After all, Jesus did say:

> But ye shall receive power, after that the Holy Ghost is come upon you: and ye shall be witnesses unto me both in Jerusalem, and in all Judaea, and in Samaria, and unto the uttermost part of the earth (Acts 1:8).

Although we are very much in miniature and filled with imperfections, God is revealing Jesus in the individual members of His church. We are Christ's representatives on earth. This is far more than legal authority, for Christ lives in us. Paul declares that God's Spirit is forming the divine image in us:

> But we all, with open face beholding as in a glass the glory of the Lord, are changed into the same image from glory to glory, even as by the Spirit of the Lord (2 Corinthians 3:18).

This is exactly what happens when we allow the life of Christ in us to cover the irritants of life with spiritual nacre. The purpose of irritation is not to separate us from God but to allow His presence in us to form pearls so that we can become gates for others to enter the divine presence.

Irritants can either form gates of pearls or barriers of sediment. Some Christians pile up their irritations until they become the only thing in the Christian's life that others can see. Other Christians simply form pearls of spiritual beauty around these aggravations. These pearls attract others to God's church and open their hearts to God's presence.

What has happened to the couple in my church who was so wounded by a church's extreme position on divorce and remarriage and who found life and healing in Christ Jesus should not surprise anyone: They have become channels through whom others have come into the presence of Jesus. Somehow those who have been wounded through divorce gravitate to this couple. The empathy and understanding they have gained by conquering this irritant in their lives helps them to understand the depth of the problem and the way to victory.

Do you remember "Doris," who lived so many years emotionally separated from her unsaved husband while continuing to pray for his salvation? She is now a doorway for other wives who do not understand how to live with the irritant of an unsaved marriage partner. The pearl that Christ produced in Doris has become an attractive doorway into the divine presence.

Abused persons in our congregation who have learned to let the nacre of Christ's forgiveness form a pearl over this painful irritant have become doorways to the healing grace of Jesus for others who have known abuse in their lives. It is not merely their empathy that draws others to them. It is their victory in a very difficult area of life. Their pearl speaks of Jesus to others.

A victorious personal involvement is the most positive testimony and witness of Christ's saving grace and mercy we can give to the world. The world does not read the Bible. Unbelievers read Christian's lives. "Ye shall be witnesses" suggests that we are the *after* picture in God's before/after advertisement. We are the finished product. Jesus says: "Look at him. Look at her. That is what I can do. Try it!" His glorious life has turned us into pearlmakers where intruding foreign objects could well have ruined our lives. Others do not see the particle of sand or understand the process of transformation. They simply see the pearl that is produced, and they are attracted to it.

People do not come to Jesus because they love Him. They come because they need Him. This means they come out of their need, whether they come from the north, south, east or west. People who approach God from the north with their "north" problems do not need to circle around to the eastern gates. People with "east" problems will not be forced to travel west. The city has gates opened toward every point of the compass. They need only look for perfectly shaped, iridescent pearls and open their ears to the invitation from Jesus:

> Come...and let him that is athirst come. And whosoever will, let him take the water of life freely (Revelation 22:17). ○